in preparation
THE RESTORATION WITS
selected by GEORGE WOODCOCK

BYRON
for To-day

Selected and with an Introduction
by ROY FULLER

THE PORCUPINE PRESS
LONDON

FIRST PUBLISHED MCMXLVIII
BY THE PORCUPINE PRESS LIMITED
26 BLOOMSBURY WAY LONDON W.C.I
PRINTED IN GREAT BRITAIN AT
THE WHITEFRIARS PRESS LTD. TONBRIDGE

TO G.W.

In the immediate future, George, the only
   Chance of a dedication I can see
Is of another's verse, so rather meanly
   I give you Byron, Lord, instead of me.
In the next war when, crowded, I am lonely,
   Bored though excited, bound but somehow free,
Perhaps I'll write another book of lyrics ;
But now I'm very far from such hysterics.

After a war there's usually a spell
   When everyone's excited and the arts
Like morals, loosen, and do rather well.
   In France and certain other foreign parts
That rule applies to-day, but England—hell !
   Our poets have no fits but only starts ;
Their gloomy thoughts engendered by the Bomb,
Are scarce relieved by right done Uncle Tom.

Byron was wise when, after Waterloo,
   He shook the dust of England from his lameness.
And if to fight for Greece like him we're too
   Politically pure or bloody shameless,
His social and his literary view
   And that of ours have some points of sameness :
Although I hope we don't sleep with our sisters
We well could do with blistering where he blisters.

Like him we have some poets who have ratted,
   And politicians who should rouse our rage,
And certain writing Gentlemen who've batted
   (Picked for their status) tediously for an age.
But I run on—the Porcupine allotted
   Four *Juan* stanzas only to a page :
Unless I stop, dear George, there'll be one less
Of Byron—so goodbye and Godwin bless !

                         R. F.

January, 1948

CONTENTS

INTRODUCTION

ON that day in 1824 when the news of Byron's death reached Somersby—'a day when the whole world seemed to be darkened'—the juvenile Tennyson went desolately out and carved on a rock the words, 'Byron is dead.' Of the same news Mrs. Carlyle wrote : ' If they had said the sun or the moon had gone out of the heavens, it could not have struck me with the idea of a more awful and dreary blank in the creation.' That the identical sensation—' the singular, the stunning sensation,' as Lytton put it some years later—should be aroused by his death in two such dissimilar characters is some indication of the extent to which Byron had, in his short lifetime, become the embodiment of the desires, the feeling, of his age.

The spirit of an age can be grasped only intellectually by a succeeding age. In literature what once was stark reality, an ageless voice, seems to the later readers a partial view, a style. The new generations reject, as dated, or false, or irrelevant, whole tracts of the literature of the past. And so, while it is perfectly easy to realise the scope of Byron's once-enormous popularity, and even to appreciate why his poetry seemed universal, a great deal of his work has lost its spell for ever.

Byron appears to us very clearly now as a poet of two styles : as the author of *Childe Harold's Pilgrimage*, the romantic narratives and the dramas, on the one hand ; on the other, as the author of *The Vision of Judgment*, *Don Juan*, and the rest of the satirical poems. But although it is the second Byron which we value more, we ought, in order to weigh his achievement properly, to understand the first.

At the date of Waterloo Byron was twenty-seven. His precariously genteel upbringing, and the unexpected inheritance of a title and landed estates while he was still at school, had planted him firmly among the aristocracy. His intelligence made him of the Whig aristocracy—that part of the ruling class which during the Napoleonic Wars and the period of reaction that followed had left the government of England to the Tories, content for the most part merely to snipe from the redoubts of the great Whig town and country houses. It was a part of the aristocracy that was still erudite, still outspoken, in the eighteenth-

7

century tradition. The middle class was busy accumulat-
ing wealth : its characteristic ideas about morals and art
had as yet scarcely any influence. The working classes
were only just beginning to recognise themselves as having
their own particular desires, interests and organisations.
The liberating ideas of the French Revolution, the chang-
ing social relations, the reaction against the rigid literature
of the later eighteenth century, had already led to the
emergence of a new poetry.

This social and literary position in Byron's formative
years enabled him, first, to inherit a ready-made and novel
romantic tradition, and secondly, to look back to the
Augustans and comment with Pope's freedom on the
personalities and ideas of his own times.

The ease with which Byron assumed the romantic cloak
is important. His satire has many gibes at Wordsworth,
Coleridge and Scott, but in *Childe Harold* most of the
philosophic feeling is a Wordsworthian pantheism (sometimes embarrassing in its inferior echoes of the older poet),
and the tales in verse which followed the publication of the
first two cantos of that poem are in the style of *The Lay
of the Last Minstrel* and *Christabel*. It is precisely because
so much of Byron's romantic poetry is in that way second-
hand that we find it hard to read it now : conversely, that
very quality made it immensely acceptable in its own time—
that and Byron's own personality. The horse-faced
Collector of Stamps for Westmorland, supremely the
conscious literary artist, could never appeal to the fashionable Regency society, still less to the would-be fashionable
sons and daughters of the new bourgeoisie ; but Byron,
much travelled, titled, pale, handsome, diabolical, carelessly dashing off his poems at preternatural speed in the
small hours after a London rout, suddenly made the
romantic revival real.

He has, I suppose, made it real to some part of every
generation since. But we need not read him only when
we are young. Byron's death ushered in a great age of
prose : poetry became entirely romantic, more and more
specialised, and finally degenerate. Byron became distor-
ted. We can see the distortion beginning as early as 1833,
in Lytton's *England and the English*. In that remarkable
work Lytton has a long passage about the ' dark and
meditative genius of Byron.' Those adjectives are

8

significant, for Lytton was young enough to have seen in Byron's romantic verse the full expression of the *zeitgeist*. But by 1833 he was feeling the pressure of bourgeois ideas : his instinctive epithets are followed by a closely reasoned argument that Byron's best work is his dramas, far superior to *Childe Harold* and the narratives, because they display not merely passion, but the ' *struggles* of passion.' Lytton is trying to find in Byron something that will make him *persona grata* to the commencing Victorian age ; he is looking for what is becoming congenial—the delineation of character and stern moral conflict.

Similarly, when Arnold, in the 'eighties, comes to assess Byron, it is the high-lights of his verse he takes mainly into account—those isolated passages where Byron has the poetic skill, the intense feeling, the sharp eye, the adroitness with words, of the best of Wordsworth or Keats. Arnold is attempting to make Byron acceptable to the cultivated man of the mature Victorian age, whose taste in poetry is already a little precious.

If, in our own times, we appreciate Byron primarily as a satirical poet it can, of course, be said against us that we are distorting Byron just as much as Lytton or Arnold. And within limits such a charge is valid. But we have Byron in far better perspective than Lytton, who was too near his romantic side, and Arnold, who was too far away from a satirical tradition. We now value highly both Wordsworth and Pope, and that gives us some right, I think, to relegate Byron's romantic verse to literary history, and to recognise, even rediscover, his satire (and by that I mean, primarily, *Don Juan*) as a novel and brilliant extension of a major mode of English poetry which under the Victorians withered away.

Byron's romantic verse bears to his achievement as a whole about the same relationship as do the details of his private life. It is absorbingly interesting to try to ascertain whether Byron's erotic tastes offended our criminal law, or to trace his wanderings about Europe and his relations with his wife and mistresses, but such things have limited relevance to *The Vision of Judgment* or *Don Juan*. His skull-cap, his bottles of claret, his quarts of magnesia, his boys, girls, and menageries, have a place in the assessment, but it is a minor one and has been exaggerated.

Nor ought one, I think, to make too much of Byron as a

revolutionary figure : he had not the temperament for politics, though he was physically courageous, and consistent in his antipathy towards reaction. Like so many other poets who derived much of their impetus from the French Revolution, he sympathised with most of the movements towards freedom of his time which he could distinguish. He sympathised with the Luddites : he was shocked by the state of the working classes in the industrial north. But there was only a rudimentary English working-class movement, and it was with a foreign struggle for liberation that in the end he identified himself. Indeed, had he been born earlier he might, like Wordsworth and Southey, have ratted on revolution : and had he been born later or lived longer it is improbable that he would have been (with Morris) the exception among English Victorian poets, comprehended the ' historical movement as a whole,' and attached himself to the struggles of the proletariat.

Byron, as I have implied, was enabled to reach his stature as a satirist through the very nature of English society during the last years of the Napoleonic Wars and the first repressive years of the peace which followed them. The aristocratic Whig society which he had entered was not only antipathetic to the ruling Tories, but often to the war itself. Byron's comment, for example, on the news of Waterloo was : ' I am damned sorry for it. I didn't know but I might live to see Lord Castlereagh's head on a pole. But I suppose I shan't now.' And his satire is not only without Tory inhibitions but also without bourgeois inhibitions. The bourgeois crust of faith or honest doubt, of belief in marital love as a way of salvation, of patriotism, of refinement, of money-making as a virtue, had not yet formed over the mind of the English artist. Byron's satire is atheistical, vulgar, irreverent, republican.

> But never mind :—' God save the king ! ' and kings !
>   For if *he* don't, I doubt if *men* will longer—
> I think I hear a little bird, who sings
>   The people by and by will be the stronger :
> The veriest jade will wince whose harness wrings
>   So much into the raw as quite to wrong her
> Beyond the rules of posting,—and the mob
> At last fall sick of imitating Job.

By the side of him a satirist of the bourgeois age, like

Clough, looks like a timid undergraduate in the college magazine.

This is not to say that *Don Juan* was acceptable to large sections of the society of its time—on the contrary. The trouble Byron had with John Murray, who wanted the strongest passage cut, and the fugitive publication of some of the cantos, was typical. But Byron *had* a large audience and he had lived in and felt himself part of a cultivated society—although it was a society that was rapidly disintegrating. How significant is the report of him in Italy when he was composing the middle cantos of *Juan*, talking old scandal, using old slang, relating anecdotes of pugilists and gamblers of his London period of 1811–16, a period which already was beginning to be historical.

But the audience and society of those most famous years were surely responsible for what is the supreme triumph of *Don Juan*—the easy, conversational, contemporary tone of the verse—a tone which had not been heard since Pope, and which has only been heard since Byron through the strenuous pioneer efforts of Mr. Eliot.

> I perch upon an humbler promontory,
>   Amidst life's infinite variety :
> With no great care for what is nicknamed glory,
>   But speculating as I cast mine eye
> On what may suit or may not suit my story
>   And never straining hard to versify,
> I rattle on exactly as I'd talk
> With any body in a ride or walk.

Everything can go into *Don Juan*—chamber-pots, galvanism, ' The Isles of Greece', topography, metaphysics, Southey, the wars—just as everything (rather more self-consciously) can go into Auden's verse.

In making the selection of Byron's poetry which follows, I have, as the foregoing remarks will have indicated, been severe with the romantic verse. I have excluded all Byron's shorter poems except some satirical and comic ones. Many of these are squibs, introduced casually into letters, and Byron took no more care over them than he did over the longer poems. Indeed, in the short poems his casualness is at its most disadvantageous : why did he not cut, and work over, that almost decent poem ' The Irish

Avatar,' or finish 'The Devil's Drive' which begins so promisingly :

> The Devil return'd to hell by two,
> And he stayed at home till five ;
> When he dined on some homicides done in *ragoût*
> And a rebel or so in an *Irish stew*,
> And sausages made of a self-slain Jew—— ?

Although shortage of space has played some part in the omission of the more serious short poems, I must confess that the love poems and the lyrics for music do not make any great appeal to me. In pieces like 'She walks in Beauty, like the night' and 'There be none of Beauty's daughters' all the magic is in the first line : the rest is melodious and accomplished, but no better than the general level of lyric writing of the period. In general, Byron had not the talent for the short poem which continues to stun one, although I was tempted to include one or two poems which throughout bear the mark of strong emotion, like the one about Lady Caroline Lamb beginning 'Remember thee ! Remember thee !'. Hackneyed poems such as 'The Destruction of Sennacherib' I have rejected mainly because they are easily accessible in anthologies.

Nor are the romantic narratives represented. From these dashing poems—particularly *The Siege of Corinth*—one could no doubt select some very passable lines. But I feel that anyone who wants to read them now should read them as wholes. Their general level can be easily and accurately ascertained by picking a passage at random :

> The walls grew weak ; and fast and hot
> Against them pour'd the ceaseless shot,
> With unabating fury sent
> From battery to battlement ;
> And thunder-like the pealing din
> Rose from each heated culverin.

The romantic poem of Byron's which deserves and can bear excision is *Childe Harold's Pilgrimage*. It was not conceived as a whole (the first two cantos were written in 1809 and 1810, during Byron's first tour abroad : the third and fourth after he had gone abroad for the second time in 1816) and it falls, by its very nature, into fairly clearly defined sections. Cantos I and II, publication of

which made Byron famous over-night, have principally
a curiosity value. It needs a good deal of imagination to
conceive how these monotonous Spenserian stanzas made
their terrific effect in 1812. For they still employ the
tepid, later-eighteenth-century diction ('soft,' 'jocund,'
'lusty,' 'cheer,' 'trembling,' one finds in a few consecutive
lines), and sometimes a shame-making older archaism (like
'ne' and 'ee'). Even their establishment of the Byronic
character must seem to us now singularly unforceful :

> Few earthly things found favour in his sight
> Save concubines and carnal companie . . .
> With pleasure drugg'd, he almost long'd for woe . . .
> Where Superstition once had made her den
> Now Paphian girls were known to sing and smile . . .
> For he through Sin's long labyrinth had run . . .

From such lines we get an impression of little more than a
provincial and largely theoretical naughtiness.

But even in Cantos I and II there are vivid flashes which
illuminate the Europe of the time :

> The mountain-howitzer, the broken road,
> The bristling palisade, the fosse o'erflow'd,
> The station'd bands, the never-vacant watch . . .

and eloquent outbursts about war and freedom which have
a special meaning for our own age. Accordingly, I have
included three of such passages in my selection.

Cantos III and IV are another matter. They were
written when the Napoleonic Wars were over, during the
first reactionary years of the peace. Byron had fled abroad
after the scandalous break-up of his marriage. And he had,
since writing the first two cantos, been reading Wordsworth's *Excursion* and clearly with attention. The change
is apparent right at the start of Canto III. The deep
feeling has resulted in enjambment : the formal stanza has
become personal : the eighteenth century has been left far
behind :

> 'T is to create, and in creating live
> A being more intense, that we endow
> With form our fancy, gaining as we give
> The life we image . . .

With all their faults, these two cantos obviously consti-
tute a great poem, and I hope I have not damaged it—

perhaps I have even rendered it more acceptable—by the very large excisions I have had to make in presenting it here.

As I have said already, Byron's satire derived in the first place directly from Pope. *English Bards and Scotch Reviewers* (which he wrote as a counterblast to the critics who were unkind to his first book), and its sequel, *Hints from Horace*, are entirely Popean. They are both disappointing poems, though the *English Bards* impudently and brightly blows raspberries at all the most distinguished living poets without the slightest discrimination. As a specimen, I have chosen a passage which seemed particularly apt in the present state of English verse. I have also printed part of a not unamusing poem called 'The Waltz,' which was written the year after the *Hints*, in 1812. In this period piece there are signs that Byron is beginning to loosen up the rigid Popean form.

But the characteristic Byronesque satirical style does not appear until *Beppo*, which was composed in 1817. I would have liked to have included *Beppo* in this selection, but space forbade. It is far from completely successful, but it does make a landmark in Byron's poetical progress. All the digression, much of the splendid ease, of *Don Juan* are there, and so is the sane and civilised tone. The style had a curious genesis. 'I have written,' Byron informed Murray about *Beppo*, 'a poem humorous, in or after the excellent manner of Mr. Whistlecraft.' Byron was referring to a poem by John Hookham Frere called 'Prospectus and Specimen of an Intended National Work, by William and Robert Whistlecraft, of Stowmarket in Suffolk, Harness and Collar Makers, intended to comprise the most interesting Particulars relating to King Arthur and his Round Table' (1817–18). Frere himself had taken his idea from the Italian poet Berni and his precursor Pulci. 'Whistlecraft is my immediate model,' said Byron, 'but Berni is the father of that kind of writing ; which, I think, suits our language, too, very well.' In Byron's hands it did indeed : the stanza, laconic narrative, and commentary of Frere's forgotten poem proved to be precisely the formal stimulus which his feeling and ideas required, and he transformed them into quite a new kind of poetry. The casual, comic, corruscating style was taken up again five years later for *The Vision of Judgment*, and Whistlecraft received his apotheosis in *Don Juan*, which dates from the last years of Byron's life.

The Vision of Judgment seems to me the best complete poem which Byron ever wrote, and I have therefore printed it entire. I have puzzled a good deal as to the best manner in which to deal with *Don Juan*. I had room for rather more than 2,000 lines, and that seemed obviously to indicate one canto complete to fill the bulk of the space. One of the main points of *Juan* is its ability to turn from one subject to another, on several levels, weaving round the narrative, and to start to cut is to start to destroy the point. But which canto ought I to choose ? I think there is little doubt that the best cantos are II and III, but for my purpose I considered that Canto II had rather too much narrative, and that Canto III was somewhat hackneyed. The English cantos at the end of the poem are not, I think, as well known as the others, but a single one of them cannot very well be detached. A canto from the middle would scarcely have suited a reader fresh to *Juan*. Accordingly, I have taken the line of least resistance and printed the first canto : it is brilliant, it requires no introductory explanation about the story, and I hope it will lead new readers on to the poem as a whole. The short extracts from five of the other cantos which follow (chosen for their excellence, or because they are topical again, or for both reasons) will give such readers some taste of its general quality.

Byron's dramas I have considered (conveniently) as outside the scope of this little book : they are rich, at least, in psychological material. My selection ends with some extracts from the letters, made to throw light on the poems rather than on the life : I hope that, incidentally, they show some of the unique and splendid qualities of Byron's prose.

ROY FULLER

15

CANTO I

Omitted stanzas are indicated thus .

*

XXXIX

Lo ! where the Giant [1] on the mountain stands,
His blood-red tresses deep'ning in the sun,
With death-shot glowing in his fiery hands,
And eye that scorcheth all it glares upon ;
Restless it rolls, now fix'd, and now anon
Flashing afar,—and at his iron feet
Destruction cowers, to mark what deeds are done ;
For on this morn three potent nations meet,
To shed before his shrine the blood he deems most sweet.

XL

By Heaven ! it is a splendid sight to see
(For one who hath no friend, no brother there)
Their rival scarfs of mix'd embroidery,
Their various arms that glitter in the air !
What gallant war-hounds rouse them from their lair,
And gnash their fangs, loud yelling for the prey !
All join the chase, but few the triumphs share ;
The Grave shall bear the chiefest prize away,
And Havoc scarce for joy can number their array.

XLI

Three hosts combine to offer sacrifice ;
Three tongues prefer strange orisons on high ;
Three gaudy standards flout the pale blue skies ;
The shouts are France, Spain, Albion, Victory !
The foe, the victim, and the fond ally
That fights for all, but ever fights in vain,
Are met—as if at home they could not die—
To feed the crow on Talavera's plain,
And fertilize the field that each pretends to gain.

[1] A personification of battle—R.F.

XLII

There shall they rot—Ambition's honour'd fools.
Yes, Honour decks the turf that wraps their clay ;
Vain Sophistry ! in these behold the tools,
The broken tools, that tyrants cast away
By myriads, when they dare to pave their way
With human hearts—to what ?—a dream alone.
Can despots compass aught that hails their sway ?
Or call with truth one span of earth their own,
Save that wherein at last they crumble bone by bone ?

*

XLIX

On yon long, level plain, at distance crown'd
With crags, whereon those Moorish turrets rest,
Wide scatter'd hoof-marks dint the wounded ground ;
And, scathed by fire, the greensward's darken'd vest
Tells that the foe was Andalusia's guest :
Here was the camp, the watch-flame, and the host,
Here the bold peasant storm'd the dragon's nest ;
Still does he mark it with triumphant boast ;
And points to yonder cliffs, which oft were won and lost.

L

And whomsoe'er along the path you meet
Bears in his cap the badge of crimson hue,
Which tells you whom to shun and whom to greet.
Woe to the man who walks in public view
Without of loyalty this token true :
Sharp is the knife, and sudden is the stroke ;
And sorely would the Gallic foeman rue,
If subtle poniards, wrapt beneath the cloke,
Could blunt the sabre's edge, or clear the cannon's smoke.

LI

At every turn Morena's dusky height
Sustains aloft the battery's iron load ;
And, far as mortal eye can compass sight,
The mountain-howitzer, the broken road,
The bristling palisade, the fosse o'erflow'd,
The station'd bands, the never-vacant watch,
The magazine in rocky durance stow'd,
The holster'd steed beneath the shed of thatch,
The ball-piled pyramid, the ever-blazing match,

Portend the deeds to come :—but he whose nod
Has tumbled feebler despots from their sway,
A moment pauseth ere he lifts the rod ;
A little moment deigneth to delay :
Soon will his legions sweep through these their way ;
The West must own the Scourger of the world.
Ah ! Spain ! how sad will be thy reckoning day,
When soars Gaul's Vulture, with his wings unfurl'd,
And thou shalt view thy sons in crowds to Hades hurl'd.

*

CANTO II

LXXIII

Fair Greece ! sad relic of departed worth !
Immortal, though no more ; though fallen, great !
Who now shall lead thy scatter'd children forth,
And long accustom'd bondage uncreate ?
Not such thy sons who whilome did await,
The hopeless warriors of a willing doom,
In bleak Thermopylæ's sepulchral strait—
Oh ! who that gallant spirit shall resume,
Leap from Eurota's banks, and call thee from the tomb ?

LXXIV

Spirit of freedom ! when on Phyle's brow
Thou sat'st with Thrasybulus and his train,
Couldst thou forbode the dismal hour which now
Dims the green beauties of thine Attic plain ?
Not thirty tyrants now enforce the chain,
But every carle can lord it o'er thy land ;
Nor rise thy sons, but idly rail in vain,
Trembling beneath the scourge of Turkish hand ;
From birth till death enslaved ; in word, in deed, unmann'd.

LXXV

In all save form alone, how changed ! and who
That marks the fire still sparkling in each eye,
Who would but deem their bosoms burn'd anew
With thy unquenched beam, lost Liberty !
And many dream withal the hour is nigh
That gives them back their fathers' heritage :
For foreign arms and aid they fondly sigh,
Nor solely dare encounter hostile rage,
Or tear their name defiled from Slavery's mournful page.

Hereditary bondsmen ! know ye not
Who would be free themselves must strike the blow ?
By their right arms the conquest must be wrought ?
Will Gaul or Muscovite redress ye ? no !
True they may lay your proud despoilers low,
But not for you will Freedom's altars flame.
Shades of the Helots ! triumph o'er your foe !
Greece ! change thy lords, thy state is still the same ;
Thy glorious day is o'er, but not thy years of shame.

*

CANTO III

XVIII

And Harold stands upon this place of skulls,
The grave of France, the deadly Waterloo !
How in an hour the power which gave annuls
Its gifts, transferring fame as fleeting too !
In ' pride of place ' here last the eagle flew,
Then tore with bloody talon the rent plain,
Pierced by the shaft of banded nations through ;
Ambition's life and labours all were vain ;
He wears the shatter'd links of the world's broken chain.

XIX

Fit retribution ! Gaul may champ the bit
And foam in fetters ;—but is Earth more free ?
Did nations combat to make *One* submit ;
Or league to teach all kings true sovereignty ?
What ! shall reviving Thraldom again be
The patch'd-up idol of enlighten'd days ?
Shall we, who struck the Lion down, shall we
Pay the Wolf homage ? proffering lowly gaze
And servile knees to thrones ? No ; *prove* before ye praise

XX

If not, o'er one fallen despot boast no more !
In vain fair cheeks were furrow'd with hot tears
For Europe's flowers long rooted up before
The trampler of her vineyards ; in vain years
Of death, depopulation, bondage, fears,
Have all been borne, and broken by the accord
Of roused-up millions ; all that most endears
Glory, is when the myrtle wreaths a sword
Such as Harmodius drew on Athens' tyrant lord.

There was a sound of revelry by night,
And Belgium's capital had gather'd then
Her Beauty and her Chivalry, and bright
The lamps shone o'er fair women and brave men ;
A thousand hearts beat happily ; and when
Music arose with its voluptuous swell,
Soft eyes look'd love to eyes which spake again,
And all went merry as a marriage bell ;
But hush ! hark ! a deep sound strikes like a rising knell !

XXII

Did ye not hear it ?—No ; 't was but the wind,
Or the car rattling o'er the stony street ;
On with the dance ! let joy be unconfined ;
No sleep till morn, when Youth and Pleasure meet
To chase the glowing Hours with flying feet—
But hark !—that heavy sound breaks in once more,
As if the clouds its echo would repeat ;
And nearer, clearer, deadlier than before !
Arm ! Arm ! it is—it is—the cannon's opening roar !

XXIII

Within a window'd niche of that high hall
Sate Brunswick's fated chieftain ; he did hear
That sound the first amidst the festival,
And caught its tone with Death's prophetic ear ;
And when they smiled because he deem'd it near,
His heart more truly knew that peal too well
Which stretch'd his father on a bloody bier,
And roused the vengeance blood alone could quell ;
He rush'd into the field, and, foremost fighting, fell.

XXIV

Ah ! then and there was hurrying to and fro,
And gathering tears, and tremblings of distress,
And cheeks all pale, which but an hour ago
Blush'd at the praise of their own loveliness ;
And there were sudden partings, such as press
The life from out young hearts, and choking sighs
Which ne'er might be repeated ; who could guess
If ever more should meet those mutual eyes,
Since upon night so sweet such awful morn could rise !

XXV

And there was mounting in hot haste : the steed,
The mustering squadron, and the clattering car,
Went pouring forward with impetuous speed,
And swiftly forming in the ranks of war ;
And the deep thunder peal on peal afar ;
And near, the beat of the alarming drum
Roused up the soldier ere the morning star ;
While throng'd the citizens with terror dumb,
Or whispering with white lips—' The foe ! they come ! they
    come !'

XXVI

And wild and high the ' Cameron's gathering ' rose !
The war-note of Lochiel, which Albyn's hills
Have heard, and heard, too, have her Saxon foes :—
How in the noon of night that pibroch thrills,
Savage and shrill ! But with the breath which fills
Their mountain pipe, so fill the mountaineers
With the fierce native daring which instils
The stirring memory of a thousand years,
And Evan's, Donald's fame rings in each clansman's ears !

XXVII

And Ardennes waves above them her green leaves,
Dewy with nature's tear-drops as they pass,
Grieving, if aught inanimate e'er grieves,
Over the unreturning brave,—alas !
Ere evening to be trodden like the grass
Which now beneath them, but above shall grow
In its next verdure, when this fiery mass
Of living valour, rolling on the foe
And burning with high hope shall moulder cold and low.

XXVIII

Last noon beheld them full of lusty life,
Last eve in Beauty's circle proudly gay,
The midnight brought the signal-sound of strife,
The morn the marshalling in arms,—the day
Battle's magnificently stern array !
The thunder-clouds close o'er it, which when rent
The earth is cover'd thick with other clay,
Which her own clay shall cover, heap'd and pent,
Rider and horse,—friend, foe,—in one red burial blent !

Their praise is hymn'd by loftier harps than mine :
Yet one I would select from that proud throng,
Partly because they blend me with his line,
And partly that I did his sire some wrong,
And partly that bright names will hallow song ;
And his was of the bravest, and when shower'd
The death-bolts deadliest the thinn'd files along,
Even where the thickest of war's tempest lower'd,
They reach'd no nobler breast than thine, young gallant
    Howard !

There have been tears and breaking hearts for thee,
And mine were nothing had I such to give ;
But when I stood beneath the fresh green tree,
Which living waves where thou didst cease to live,
And saw around me the wide field revive
With fruits and fertile promise, and the Spring
Came forth her work of gladness to contrive,
With all her reckless birds upon the wing,
I turn'd from all she brought to those she could not bring.

I turn'd to thee, to thousands, of whom each
And one as all a ghastly gap did make
In his own kind and kindred, whom to teach
Forgetfulness were mercy for their sake ;
The Archangel's trump, not Glory's, must awake
Those whom they thirst for ; though the sound of Fame
May for a moment soothe, it cannot slake
The fever of vain longing, and the name
So honour'd but assumes a stronger, bitterer claim.

They mourn, but smile at length ; and, smiling, mourn :
The tree will wither long before it fall ;
The hull drives on, though mast and sail be torn ;
The roof-tree sinks, but moulders on the hall
In massy hoariness ; the ruin'd wall
Stands when its wind-worn battlements are gone ;
The bars survive the captive they enthral ;
The day drags through, though storms keep out the sun ;
And thus the heart will break, yet brokenly live on :

Even as a broken mirror, which the glass
In every fragment multiplies ; and makes
A thousand images of one that was,
The same, and still the more, the more it breaks ;
And thus the heart will do which not forsakes,
Living in shatter'd guise ; and still, and cold,
And bloodless, with its sleepless sorrow aches,
Yet withers on till all without is old,
Showing no visible sign, for such things are untold.

There is a very life in our despair,
Vitality of poison,—a quick root
Which feeds these deadly branches ; for it were
As nothing did we die ; but Life will suit
Itself to Sorrow's most detested fruit,
Like to the apples on the Dead Sea's shore,
All ashes to the taste : Did man compute
Existence by enjoyment, and count o'er
Such hours 'gainst years of life,—say, would he name three
    score ?

The Psalmist number'd out the years of man :
They are enough ; and if thy tale be *true*,
Thou, who didst grudge him even that fleeting span,
More than enough, thou fatal Waterloo !
Millions of tongues record thee, and anew
Their children's lips shall echo them, and say—
' Here, where the sword united nations drew,
Our countrymen were warring on that day ! '
And this is much, and all which will not pass away.

There sunk the greatest, nor the worst of men,
Whose spirit, antithetically mixt,
One moment of the mightiest, and again
On little objects with like firmness fixt ;
Extreme in all things ! hadst thou been betwixt,
Thy throne had still been thine, or never been ;
For daring made thy rise as fall : thou seek'st
Even now to re-assume the imperial mien,
And shake again the world, the Thunderer of the scene !

Conqueror and captive of the earth art thou !
She tremblest at thee still, and thy wild name
Was ne'er more bruited in men's minds than now
That thou art nothing, save the jest of Fame,
Who woo'd thee once, thy vassal, and became
The flatterer of thy fierceness, till thou wert
A god unto thyself ; nor less the same
To the astounded kingdoms all inert,
Who deem'd thee for a time whate'er thou didst assert.

Oh, more or less than man—in high or low,
Battling with nations, flying from the field ;
Now making monarchs' necks thy footstool, now
More than thy meanest soldier taught to yield ;
An empire thou couldst crush, command, rebuild,
But govern not thy pettiest passion, nor
However deeply in men's spirits skill'd,
Look through thine own, nor curb the lust of war,
Nor learn that tempted Fate will leave the loftiest star.

Yet well thy soul hath brook'd the turning tide
With that untaught innate philosophy,
Which, be it wisdom, coldness, or deep pride,
Is gall and wormwood to an enemy.
When the whole host of hatred stood hard by,
To watch and mock thee shrinking, thou hast smiled
With a sedate and all-enduring eye ;—
When Fortune fled her spoil'd and favourite child,
He stood unbow'd beneath the ills upon him piled.

Sager than in thy fortunes ; for in them
Ambition steel'd thee on too far to show
That just habitual scorn, which could contemn
Men and their thoughts ; 't was wise to feel, not so
To wear it ever on thy lip and brow,
And spurn the instruments thou wert to use
Till they were turn'd unto thine overthrow :
'T is but a worthless world to win or lose ;
So hath it proved to thee, and all such lot who choose.

If, like a tower upon a headland rock,
Thou hadst been made to stand or fall alone,
Such scorn of man had help'd to brave the shock
But men's thoughts were the steps which paved thy throne,
Their admiration thy best weapon shone :
The part of Philip's son was thine, not then
(Unless aside thy purple had been thrown)
Like stern Diogenes to mock at men ;
For sceptred cynics earth were far too wide a den.

XLII

But quiet to quick bosoms is a hell,
And *there* hath been thy bane ; there is a fire
And motion of the soul which will not dwell
In its own narrow being, but aspire
Beyond the fitting medium of desire ;
And, but once kindled, quenchless evermore,
Preys upon high adventure, nor can tire
Of aught but rest ; a fever at the core,
Fatal to him who bears, to all who ever bore.

XLIII

This makes the madmen who have made men mad
By their contagion ; Conquerors and Kings,
Founders of sects and systems, to whom add
Sophists, Bards, Statesmen, all unquiet things
Which stir too strongly the soul's secret springs,
And are themselves the fools to those they fool ;
Envied, yet how unenviable ! what stings
Are theirs ! One breast laid open were a school
Which would unteach mankind the lust to shine or rule :

XLIV

Their breath is agitation, and their life
A storm whereon they ride, to sink at last,
And yet so nursed and bigoted to strife,
That should their days, surviving perils past,
Melt to calm twilight, they feel overcast
With sorrow and supineness, and so die ;
Even as a flame unfed, which runs to waste
With its own flickering or a sword laid by,
Which eats into itself, and rusts ingloriously.

XLV

He who ascends to mountain-tops, shall find
The loftiest peaks most wrapt in clouds and snow ;
He who surpasses or subdues mankind,
Must look down on the hate of those below
Though high *above* the sun of glory glow,
And far *beneath* the earth and ocean spread,
Round him are icy rocks, and loudly blow
Contending tempests on his naked head,
And thus reward the toils which to those summits led.

*

LXII

But these recede. Above me are the Alps,
The palaces of Nature, whose vast walls
Have pinnacled in clouds their snowy scalps,
And throned Eternity in icy halls
Of cold sublimity, where forms and falls
The avalanche—the thunderbolt of snow !
All that expands the spirit, yet appals,
Gather around these summits, as to show
How Earth may pierce to Heaven, yet leave vain man below.

LXIII

But ere these matchless heights I dare to scan,
There is a spot should not be pass'd in vain,—
Morat ! the proud, the patriot field ! where man
May gaze on ghastly trophies of the slain,
Nor blush for those who conquer'd on that plain ;
Here Burgundy bequeath'd his tombless host,
A bony heap, through ages to remain,
Themselves their monument ;—the Stygian coast
Unsepulchred they roam'd, and shriek'd each wandering
    ghost.

LXIV

While Waterloo with Cannæ's carnage vies,
Morat and Marathon twin names shall stand ;
They were true Glory's stainless victories,
Won by the unambitious heart and hand
Of a proud, brotherly, and civic band,
All unbought champions in no princely cause
Of vice-entail'd Corruption ; they no land
Doom'd to bewail the blasphemy of laws
Making kings' rights divine, by some Draconic clause.

27

LXV

By a lone wall a lonelier column rears
A gray and grief-worn aspect of old days;
'T is the last remnant of the wreck of years,
And looks as with the wild-bewilder'd gaze
Of one to stone converted by amaze,
Yet still with consciousness; and there it stands
Making a marvel that it not decays,
When the coeval pride of human hands,
Levell'd Adventicum, hath strew'd her subject lands.

LXVI

And there—oh! sweet and sacred be the name!—
Julia—the daughter, the devoted—gave
Her youth to Heaven; her heart, beneath a claim
Nearest to Heaven's, broke o'er a father's grave.
Justice is sworn 'gainst tears, and hers would crave
The life she lived in; but the judge was just,
And then she died on him she could not save.
Their tomb was simple, and without a bust,
And held within their urn one mind, one heart, one dust.

LXVII

But these are deeds which should not pass away,
And names that must not wither, though the earth
Forgets her empires with a just decay,
The enslavers and the enslaved, their death and birth;
The high, the mountain-majesty of worth
Should be, and shall, survivor of its woe,
And from its immortality look forth
In the sun's face, like yonder Alpine snow,
Imperishably pure beyond all things below.

LXVIII

Lake Leman woos me with its crystal face,
The mirror where the stars and mountains view
The stillness of their aspect in each trace
Its clear depth yields of their far height and hue:
There is too much of man here, to look through
With a fit mind the might which I behold;
But soon in me shall Loneliness renew
Thoughts hid, but not less cherish'd than of old,
Ere mingling with the herd had penn'd me in their fold.

To fly from, need not be to hate, mankind:
All are not fit with them to stir and toil,
Nor is it discontent to keep the mind
Deep in its fountain, lest it overboil
In the hot throng, where we become the spoil
Of our infection, till too late and long
We may deplore and struggle with the coil,
In wretched interchange of wrong for wrong
Midst a contentious world, striving where none are strong.

There, in a moment we may plunge our years
In fatal penitence, and in the blight
Of our own soul turn all our blood to tears,
And colour things to come with hues of Night;
The race of life becomes a hopeless flight
To those that walk in darkness: on the sea
The boldest steer but where their ports invite;
But there are wanderers o'er Eternity
Whose bark drives on and on, and anchor'd ne'er shall be.

Is it not better, then, to be alone,
And love Earth only for its earthly sake?
By the blue rushing of the arrowy Rhone,
Or the pure bosom of its nursing lake,
Which feeds it as a mother who doth make
A fair but froward infant her own care,
Kissing its cries away as these awake;—
Is it not better thus our lives to wear,
Than join the rushing crowd, doom'd to inflict or bear?

I live not in myself, but I become
Portion of that around me; and to me
High mountains are a feeling, but the hum
Of human cities torture: I can see
Nothing to loathe in nature, save to be
A link reluctant in a fleshly chain,
Class'd among creatures, when the soul can flee
And with the sky, the peak, the heaving plain
Of ocean, or the stars, mingle, and not in vain.

And thus I am absorb'd, and this is life :
I look upon the peopled desert past,
As on a place of agony and strife,
Where, for some sin, to sorrow I was cast,
To act and suffer, but remount at last
With a fresh pinion ; which I feel to spring,
Though young, yet waxing vigorous as the blast
Which it would cope with, on delighted wing,
Spurning the clay-cold bonds which round our being cling.

And when, at length, the mind shall be all free
From what it hates in this degraded form,
Reft of its carnal life, save what shall be
Existent happier in the fly and worm,—
When elements to elements conform,
And dust is as it should be, shall I not
Feel all I see, less dazzling, but more warm ?
The bodiless thought ? the Spirit of each spot ?
Of which, even now, I share at times the immortal lot ?

Are not the mountains, waves, and skies, a part
Of me and of my soul, as I of them ?
Is not the love of these deep in my heart
With a pure passion ? should I not contemn
All objects, if compared with these ? and stem
A tide of suffering, rather than forego
Such feelings for the hard and worldly phlegm
Of those whose eyes are only turn'd below,
Gazing upon the ground, with thoughts which dare not glow ?

But this is not my theme ; and I return
To that which is immediate, and require
Those who find contemplation in the urn,
To look on One, whose dust was once all fire,
A native of the land where I respire
The clear air for a while—a passing guest,
Where he became a being,—whose desire
Was to be glorious ; 't was a foolish quest
The which to gain and keep, he sacrificed all rest.

Here the self-torturing sophist, wild Rousseau,
The apostle of affliction, he who threw
Enchantment over passion, and from woe
Wrung overwhelming eloquence, first drew
The breath which made him wretched ; yet he knew
How to make madness beautiful, and cast
O'er erring deeds and thoughts a heavenly hue
Of words, like sunbeams, dazzling as they past
The eyes, which o'er them shed tears feelingly and fast.

LXXVIII

His love was passion's essence :—as a tree
On fire by lightning, with ethereal flame
Kindled he was, and blasted ; for to be
Thus and enamour'd, were in him the same.
But his was not the love of living dame,
Nor of the dead who rise upon our dreams,
But of ideal beauty, which became
In him existence, and o'erflowing teems
Along his burning page, distemper'd though it seems.

LXXIX

This breathed itself to life in Julie, *this*
Invested her with all that's wild and sweet ;
This hallow'd, too, the memorable kiss
Which every morn his fever'd lip would greet,
From hers, who but with friendship his would meet ;
But to that gentle touch through brain and breast
Flash'd the thrill'd spirit's love-devouring heat ;
In that absorbing sigh perchance more blest
Than vulgar minds may be with all they seek possest.

LXXX

His life was one long war with self-sought foes,
Or friends by him self-banish'd ; for his mind
Had grown Suspicion's sanctuary, and chose,
For its own cruel sacrifice, the kind,
'Gainst whom he raged with fury strange and blind.
But he was phrensied,—wherefore, who may know ?
Since cause might be which skill could never find ;
But he was phrensied by disease or woe,
To that worst pitch of all, which wears a reasoning show.

LXXXI

For then he was inspired, and from him came,
As from the Pythian's mystic cave of yore,
Those oracles which set the world in flame,
Nor ceased to burn till kingdoms were no more :
Did he not this for France ? which lay before
Bow'd to the inborn tyranny of years ?
Broken and trembling to the yoke she bore,
Till by the voice of him and his compeers
Roused up to too much wrath, which follows o'ergrown fear

LXXXII

They made themselves a fearful monument !
The wreck of old opinions—things which grew,
Breathed from the birth of time : the veil they rent,
And what behind it lay, all earth shall view.
But good with ill they also overthrew,
Leaving but ruins, wherewith to rebuild
Upon the same foundation, and renew
Dungeons and thrones, which the same hour refill'd,
As heretofore, because ambition was self-will'd.

LXXXIII

But this will not endure, nor be endured !
Mankind have felt their strength, and made it felt.
They might have used it better, but, allured
By their new vigour, sternly have they dealt
On one another ; pity ceased to melt
With her once natural charities.   But they,
Who in oppression's darkness caved had dwelt,
They were not eagles, nourish'd with the day ;
What marvel then, at times, if they mistook their prey ?

LXXXIV

What deep wounds ever closed without a scar ?
The heart's bleed longest, and but heal to wear
That which disfigures it ; and they who war
With their own hopes, and have been vanquish'd, bear
Silence, but not submission ; in his lair
Fix'd Passion holds his breath, until the hour
Which shall atone for years ; none need despair :
It came, it cometh, and will come,—the power
To punish or forgive—in *one* we shall be slower.

*

But let me quit man's works, again to read
His Maker's spread around me, and suspend
This page, which from my reveries I feed,
Until it seems prolonging without end.
The clouds above me to the white Alps tend,
And I must pierce them, and survey whate'er
May be permitted, as my steps I bend
To their most great and growing region, where
he earth to her embrace compels the powers of air.

Italia ! too, Italia ! looking on thee,
Full flashes on the soul the light of ages,
Since the fierce Carthaginian almost won thee,
To the last halo of the chiefs and sages
Who glorify thy consecrated pages ;
Thou wert the throne and grave of empires ; still,
The fount at which the panting mind assuages
Her thirst of knowledge, quaffing there her fill,
ows from the eternal source of Rome's imperial hill.

Thus far have I proceeded in a theme
Renew'd with no kind auspices :—to feel
We are not what we have been, and to deem
We are not what we should be, and to steel
The heart against itself ; and to conceal,
With a proud caution, love, or hate, or aught,—
Passion or feeling, purpose, grief, or zeal,—
Which is the tyrant spirit of our thought,
a stern task of soul :—No matter,—it is taught.

And for these words, thus woven into song,
It may be that they are a harmless wile,—
The colouring of the scenes which fleet along,
Which I would seize, in passing, to beguile
My breast, or that of others, for a while.
Fame is the thirst of youth, but I am not
So young as to regard men's frown or smile,
As loss or guerdon of a glorious lot ;
tood and stand alone,—remember'd or forgot.

CXIII

I have not loved the world, nor the world me ;
I have not flatter'd its rank breath, nor bow'd
To its idolatries a patient knee,
Nor coin'd my cheek to smiles, nor cried aloud
In worship of an echo ; in the crowd
They could not deem me one of such ; I stood
Among them, but not of them ; in a shroud
Of thoughts which were not their thoughts, and still c
Had I not filed my mind, which thus itself subdued.

CXIV

I have not loved the world, nor the world me,—
But let us part fair foes ; I do believe,
Though I have found them not, that there may be
Words which are things, hopes which will not deceive
And virtues which are merciful, nor weave
Snares for the failing ; I would also deem
O'er others' griefs that some sincerely grieve ;
That two, or one, are almost what they seem,
That goodness is no name, and happiness no dream.

CANTO IV

I

I stood in Venice, on the Bridge of Sighs ;
A palace and a prison on each hand :
I saw from out the wave her structures rise
As from the stroke of the enchanter's wand :
A thousand years their cloudy wings expand
Around me, and a dying Glory smiles
O'er the far times, when many a subject land
Look'd to the winged Lion's marble piles,
Where Venice sate in state, throned on her hundred isles

II

She looks a sea Cybele, fresh from ocean,
Rising with her tiara of proud towers
At airy distance, with majestic motion,
A ruler of the waters and their powers :
And such she was :—her daughters had their dowers
From spoils of nations, and the exhaustless East
Pour'd in her lap all gems in sparkling showers.
In purple was she robed, and of her feast
Monarchs partook, and deem'd their dignity increased.

III

In Venice Tasso's echoes are no more,
And silent rows the songless gondolier ;
Her palaces are crumbling to the shore,
And music meets not always now the ear :
Those days are gone—but Beauty still is here.
States fall, arts fade—but Nature doth not die,
Nor yet forget how Venice once was dear,
The pleasant place of all festivity,
The revel of the earth, the masque of Italy !

IV

But unto us she hath a spell beyond
Her name in story, and her long array
Of mighty shadows, whose dim forms despond
Above the dogeless city's vanish'd sway ;
Ours is a trophy which will not decay
With the Rialto ; Shylock and the Moor,
And Pierre, cannot be swept or worn away—
The keystones of the arch ! though all were o'er,
For us repeopled were the solitary shore.

V

The beings of the mind are not of clay ;
Essentially immortal, they create
And multiply in us a brighter ray
And more beloved existence : that which Fate
Prohibits to dull life, in this our state
Of mortal bondage by these spirits supplied,
First exiles, then replaces what we hate ;
Watering the heart whose early flowers have died,
And with a fresher growth replenishing the void.

VI

Such is the refuge of our youth and age,
The first from Hope, the last from Vacancy ;
And this worn feeling peoples many a page,
And, may be, that which grows beneath mine eye :
Yet there are things whose strong reality
Outshines our fairy-land ; in shape and hues
More beautiful than our fantastic sky,
And the strange constellations which the Muse
O'er her wild universe is skilful to diffuse.

*

The spouseless Adriatic mourns her lord ;
And, annual marriage now no more renew'd,
The Bucentaur lies rotting unrestored,
Neglected garment of her widowhood !
St. Mark yet sees his lion where he stood
Stand, but in mockery of his wither'd power,
Over the proud Palace where an Emperor sued,
And monarchs gazed and envied in the hour
When Venice was a queen with an unequall'd dower.

XII

The Suabian sued, and now the Austrian reigns—
An Emperor tramples where an Emperor knelt ;
Kingdoms are shrunk to provinces, and chains
Clank over sceptred cities ; nations melt
From power's high pinnacle, when they have felt
The sunshine for a while, and downward go
Like lauwine loosen'd from the mountain's belt ;
Oh for one hour of blind old Dandolo !
Th' octogenarian chief, Byzantium's conquering foe.

XIII

Before St. Mark still glow his steeds of brass,
Their gilded collars glittering in the sun ;
But is not Doria's menace come to pass ?
Are they not *bridled ?*—Venice, lost and won,
Her thirteen hundred years of freedom done,
Sinks, like a seaweed, into whence she rose !
Better be whelm'd beneath the waves, and shun
Even in destruction's depth, her foreign foes,
From whom submission wrings an infamous repose.

XIV

In youth she was all glory,—a new Tyre ;
Her very by-word sprung from victory,
The ' Planter of the Lion,' which through fire
And blood she bore o'er subject earth and sea ;
Though making many slaves, herself still free,
And Europe's bulwark 'gainst the Ottomite ;
Witness Troy's rival, Candia ! Vouch it, ye
Immortal waves that saw Lepanto's fight !
For ye are names no time nor tyranny can blight.

XV

Statues of glass—all shiver'd—the long file
Of her dead Doges are declined to dust ;
But where they dwelt, the vast and sumptuous pile
Bespeaks the pageant of their splendid trust ;
Their sceptre broken, and their sword in rust,
Have yielded to the stranger : empty halls,
Thin streets, and foreign aspects, such as must
Too oft remind her who and what inthrals,
Have flung a desolate cloud o'er Venice' lovely walls.

XVI

When Athens' armies fell at Syracuse,
And fetter'd thousands bore the yoke of war,
Redemption rose up in the Attic Muse,
Her voice their only ransom from afar :
See ! as they chant the tragic hymn, the car
Of the o'ermaster'd victor stops, the reins
Fall from his hands, his idle scimitar
Starts from its belt—he rends his captive's chains,
And bids him thank the bard for freedom and his strains.

XVII

Thus, Venice, if no stronger claim were thine,
Were all thy proud historic deeds forgot,
Thy choral memory of the Bard divine,
Thy love of Tasso, should have cut the knot
Which ties thee to thy tyrants ; and thy lot
Is shameful to the nations,—most of all,
Albion ! to thee : the Ocean queen should not
Abandon Ocean's children ; in the fall
Of Venice think of thine, despite thy watery wall.

XVIII

I loved her from my boyhood ; she to me
Was as a fairy city of the heart,
Rising like water-columns from the sea,
Of joy the sojourn, and of wealth the mart ;
And Otway, Radcliffe, Schiller, Shakspeare's art,
Had stamp'd her image in me, and even so,
Although I found her thus, we did not part ;
Perchance even dearer in her day of woe,
Than when she was a boast, a marvel, and a show.

XIX

I can repeople with the past—and of
The present there is still for eye and thought,
And meditation chasten'd down, enough ;
And more, it may be, than I hoped or sought ;
And of the happiest moments which were wrought
Within the web of my existence, some
From thee, fair Venice ! have their colours caught :
There are some feelings Time cannot benumb,
Nor Torture shake, or mine would now be cold and dumb

XX

But from their nature will the tannen grow
Loftiest on loftiest and least shelter'd rocks,
Rooted in barrenness, where naught below
Of soil supports them 'gainst the Alpine shocks
Of eddying storms ; yet springs the trunk, and mocks
The howling tempest, till its height and frame
Are worthy of the mountains from whose blocks
Of bleak, gray granite into life it came,
And grew a giant tree ;—the mind may grow the same.

XXI

Existence may be borne, and the deep root
Of life and sufferance make its firm abode
The bare and desolated bosoms : mute
The camel labours with the heaviest load,
And the wolf dies in silence,—not bestow'd
In vain should such example be ; if they,
Things of ignoble or of savage mood,
Endure and shrink not, we of nobler clay
May temper it to bear,—it is but for a day.

XXII

All suffering doth destroy, or is destroy'd,
Even by the sufferer ; and, in each event,
Ends : Some, with hope replenish'd and rebuoy'd,
Return to whence they came—with like intent,
And weave their web again ; some, bow'd and bent,
Wax gray and ghastly, withering ere their time,
And perish with the reed on which they leant ;
Some seek devotion, toil, war, good or crime,
According as their souls were form'd to sink or climb.

XXIII

But ever and anon of griefs subdued
There comes a token like a scorpion's sting,
Scarce seen, but with fresh bitterness imbued ;
And slight withal may be the things which bring
Back on the heart the weight which it would fling
Aside for ever : it may be a sound—
A tone of music—summer's eve—or spring—
A flower—the wind—the ocean—which shall wound,
Striking the electric chain wherewith we are darkly bound ;

XXIV

And how and why we know not, nor can trace
Home to its cloud this lightning of the mind,
But feel the shock renew'd, nor can efface
The blight and blackening which it leaves behind,
Which out of things familiar, undesign'd,
When least we deem of such, calls up to view
The spectres whom no exorcism can bind,—
The cold, the changed, perchance the dead—anew,
The mourn'd, the loved, the lost—too many !—yet how few !

*

XCIII

What from this barren being do we reap ?
Our senses narrow, and our reason frail,
Life short, and truth a gem which loves the deep,
And all things weigh'd in custom's falsest scale ;
Opinion an omnipotence,—whose veil
Mantles the earth with darkness, until right
And wrong are accidents, and men grow pale
Lest their own judgments should become too bright,
And their free thoughts be crimes, and earth have too much
    light.

XCIV

And thus they plod in sluggish misery,
Rotting from sire to son, and age to age,
Proud of their trampled nature, and so die,
Bequeathing their hereditary rage
To the new race of inborn slaves, who wage
War for their chains, and rather than be free,
Bleed gladiator-like, and still engage
Within the same arena where they see
Their fellows fall before, like leaves of the same tree.

XCV

I speak not of men's creeds—they rest between
Man and his Maker—but of things allow'd,
Averr'd, and known, and daily, hourly seen—
The yoke that is upon us doubly bow'd,
And the intent of tyranny avow'd,
The edict of Earth's rulers, who are grown
The apes of him who humbled once the proud,
And shook them from their slumbers on the throne :
Too glorious, were this all his mighty arm had done.

XCVI

Can tyrants but by tyrants conquer'd be,
And Freedom find no champion and no child
Such as Columbia saw arise when she
Sprung forth a Pallas, arm'd and undefiled ?
Or must such minds be nourish'd in the wild,
Deep in the unpruned forest, 'midst the roar
Of cataracts, where nursing Nature smiled
On infant Washington ?   Has Earth no more
Such seeds within her breast, or Europe no such shore ?

XCVII

But France got drunk with blood to vomit crime,
And fatal have her Saturnalia been
To Freedom's cause, in every age and clime ;
Because the deadly days, which we have seen,
And vile Ambition, that built up between
Man and his hopes an adamantine wall,
And the base pageant last upon the scene,
Are grown the pretext for the eternal thrall
Which nips life's tree, and dooms man's worst—his second f

XCVIII

Yet, Freedom ! yet thy banner, torn, but flying,
Streams like the thunder-storm *against* the wind ;
Thy trumpet voice, though broken now and dying,
The loudest still the tempest leaves behind ;
Thy tree hath lost its blossoms, and the rind,
Chopp'd by the axe, looks rough and little worth,
But the sap lasts,—and still the seed we find
Sown deep, even in the bosom of the North ;
So shall a better spring less bitter fruit bring forth.

*

CVI

Then let the winds howl on ! their harmony
Shall henceforth be my music, and the night
The sound shall temper with the owlet's cry,
As I now hear them, in the fading light
Dim o'er the bird of darkness' native site,
With their large eyes, all glistening gray and bright,
And sailing pinions.—Upon such a shrine
What are our petty griefs ?—let me not number mine.

CVII

Cypress and ivy, weed and wallflower grown
Matted and mass'd together, hillocks heap'd
On what were chambers, arch crush'd, column strown
In fragments, choked up vaults, and frescos steep'd
In subterranean damps, where the owl peep'd,
Deeming it midnight :—Temples, baths, or halls ?
Pronounce who can ; for all that Learning reap'd
From her research hath been, that these are walls—
Behold the Imperial Mount ! 't is thus the mighty falls.

CVIII

There is the moral of all human tales ;
'T is but the same rehearsal of the past,
First Freedom, and then Glory—when that fails,
Wealth, vice, corruption,—barbarism at last,
And History, with all her volumes vast,
Hath but *one* page,—'t is better written here
Where gorgeous Tyranny hath thus amass'd
All treasures, all delights, that eye or ear,
Heart, soul could seek, tongue ask—Away with words ! draw
near,

CIX

Admire, exult, despise, laugh, weep,—for here
There is such matter for all feeling :—Man !
Thou pendulum betwixt a smile and tear,
Ages and realms are crowded in this span,
This mountain, whose obliterated plan
The pyramid of empires pinnacled,
Of Glory's gewgaws shining in the van
Till the sun's rays with added flame were fill'd !
Where are its golden roofs ? where those who dared to build ?

CX

Tully was not so eloquent as thou,
Thou nameless column with the buried base
What are the laurels of the Cæsar's brow?
Crown me with ivy from his dwelling-place.
Whose arch or pillar meets me in the face,
Titus or Trajan's?   No—'t is that of Time :
Triumph, arch, pillar, all he doth displace
Scoffing ; and apostolic statues climb
To crush the imperial urn, whose ashes slept sublime,

CXI

Buried in air, the deep blue sky of Rome,
And looking to the stars : they had contain'd
A spirit which with these would find a home,
The last of those who o'er the whole earth reign'd,
The Roman globe, for after none sustain'd,
But yielded back his conquests :—he was more
Than a mere Alexander, and, unstain'd
With household blood and wine, serenely wore
His sovereign virtues—still we Trajan's name adore.

*

CXL

I see before me the Gladiator lie :
He leans upon his hand—his manly brow
Consents to death, but conquers agony,
And his droop'd head sinks gradually low—
And through his side the last drops, ebbing slow
From the red gash, fall heavy, one by one,
Like the first of a thunder-shower, and now
The arena swims around him—he is gone,
Ere ceased the inhuman shout which hail'd the wretch who
    won.

CXLI

He heard it, but he heeded not—his eyes
Were with his heart, and that was far away ;
He reck'd not of the life he lost nor prize,
But where his rude hut by the Danube lay,
There were his young barbarians all at play,
There was their Dacian mother—he, their sire,
Butcher'd to make a Roman holiday—
All this rush'd with his blood—Shall he expire
And unavenged ?   Arise ! ye Goths, and glut your ire !

42

CXLII

But here, where Murder breathed her bloody steam ;
And here, where buzzing nations choked the ways,
And roar'd or murmur'd like a mountain stream
Dashing or winding as its torrent strays ;
Here, where the Roman million's blame or praise
Was death or life, the playthings of a crowd,
My voice sounds much—and fall the stars' faint rays
On the arena void—seats crush'd—walls bow'd—
And galleries, where my steps seem echoes strangely loud.

CXLIII

A ruin—yet what ruin ! from its mass
Walls, palaces, half-cities, have been rear'd ;
Yet oft the enormous skeleton ye pass,
And marvel where the spoil could have appear'd.
Hath it indeed been plunder'd, or but clear'd ?
Alas ! developed, opens the decay,
When the colossal fabric's form is near'd :
It will not bear the brightness of the day ;
Which streams too much on all years, man, have reft away.

CXLIV

But when the rising moon begins to climb
Its topmost arch, and gently pauses there ;
When the stars twinkle through the loops of time,
And the low night-breeze waves along the air
The garland-forest, which the gray walls wear,
Like laurels on the bald first Cæsar's head ;
When the light shines serene but doth not glare,
Then in this magic circle raise the dead :
Heroes have trod this spot—'t is on their dust ye tread.

CXLV

' While stands the Coliseum, Rome shall stand :
When falls the Coliseum, Rome shall fall :
And when Rome falls—the World.'   From our own land
Thus spake the pilgrims o'er this mighty wall.
In Saxon times, which we are wont to call
Ancient ; and these three mortal things are still
On their foundations, and unalter'd all ;
Rome and her Ruin past Redemption's skill,
The World the same wide den—of thieves, or what ye will.

*

CLXXVIII

There is a pleasure in the pathless woods,
There is a rapture on the lonely shore,
There is society, where none intrudes,
By the deep Sea, and music in its roar :
I love not Man the less, but Nature more,
From these our interviews, in which I steal
From all I may be, or have been before,
To mingle with the Universe, and feel
What I can ne'er express, yet cannot all conceal.

CLXXIX

Roll on, thou deep and dark blue Ocean—roll !
Ten thousand fleets sweep over thee in vain ;
Man marks the earth with ruin—his control
Stops with the shore ; upon the watery plain
The wrecks are all thy deed, nor doth remain
A shadow of man's ravage, save his own,
When, for a moment, like a drop of rain,
He sinks into thy depths with bubbling groan,
Without a grave, unknell'd, uncoffin'd, and unknown.

CLXXX

His steps are not upon thy paths,—thy fields
Are not a spoil for him,—thou dost arise
And shake him from thee ; the vile strength he wields
For earth's destruction thou dost all despise,
Spurning him from thy bosom to the skies,
And send'st him, shivering in thy playful spray
And howling, to his Gods, where haply lies
His petty hope in some near port or bay,
And dashest him again to earth :—there let him lay.

CLXXXI

The armaments which thunderstrike the walls
Of rock-built cities, bidding nations quake,
And monarchs tremble in their capitals,
The oak leviathans, whose huge ribs make
Their clay creator the vain title take
Of lord of thee, and arbiter of war—
These are thy toys, and, as the snowy flake,
They melt into thy yeast of waves, which mar
Alike the Armada's pride or spoils of Trafalgar.

Thy shores are empires, changed in all save thee—
Assyria, Greece, Rome, Carthage, what are they?
Thy waters wash'd them power while they were free,
And many a tyrant since; their shores obey
The stranger, slave, or savage; their decay
Has dried up realms to deserts:—not so thou;—
Unchangeable, save to thy wild waves' play,
Time writes no wrinkle on thine azure brow:
Such as creation's dawn beheld, thou rollest now.

Thou glorious mirror, where the Almighty's form
Glasses itself in tempests; in all time,—
Calm or convulsed, in breeze, or gale, or storm,
Icing the pole, or in the torrid clime
Dark-heaving—boundless, endless, and sublime,
The image of eternity, the throne
Of the Invisible; even from out thy slime
The monsters of the deep are made; each zone
Obeys thee; thou goest forth, dread, fathomless, alone.

*

TIME was, ere yet in these degenerate days
Ignoble themes obtain'd mistaken praise,
When sense and wit with poesy allied,
No fabled graces, flourish'd side by side ;
From the same fount their inspiration drew,
And, rear'd by taste, bloom'd fairer as they grew.
Then, in this happy isle, a Pope's pure strain
Sought the rapt soul to charm, nor sought in vain ;
A polish'd nation's praise aspired to claim,
And raised the people's, as the poet's fame.
Like him great Dryden pour'd the tide of song,
In stream less smooth, indeed, yet doubly strong.
Then Congreve's scenes could cheer or Otway's melt—
For nature then an English audience felt.
But why these names, or greater still, retrace,
When all to feebler bards resign their place ?
Yet to such times our lingering looks are cast,
When taste and reason with those times are past,
Now look around, and turn each trifling page,
Survey the precious works that please the age ;
This truth at least let satire's self allow,
No dearth of bards can be complain'd of now.
The loaded press beneath her labour groans,
And printers' devils shake their weary bones ;
While Southey's epics cram the creaking shelves,
And Little's lyrics shine in hot-press'd twelves,
Thus saith the preacher : ' Nought beneath the sun
Is new' ; yet still from change to change we run :
What varied wonders tempt us as they pass !
The cow-pox, tractors, galvanism, and gas,
In turns appear, to make the vulgar stare,
Till the swoln bubble bursts—and all is air !
Nor less new schools of Poetry arise,
Where dull pretenders grapple for the prize :
O'er taste awhile these pseudo-bards prevail ;
Each country book-club bows the knee to Baal,
And, hurling lawful genius from the throne,
Erects a shrine and idol of its own ;
Some leaden calf—but whom it matters not,
From soaring Southey down to grovelling Stott.

*

BLEST was the time Waltz chose for her *début* ;
The court, the Regent, like herself were new ;
New face for friends, for foes some new rewards ;
New ornaments for black and royal guards ;
New laws to hang the rogues that roar'd for bread ;
New coins (most new) to follow those that fled ;
New victories—nor can we prize them less,
Though Jenky wonders at his own success ;
New wars, because the old succeed so well,
That most survivors envy those who fell ;
New mistresses—no, old—and yet 't is true,
Though they be *old*, the *thing* is something new ;
Each new, quite new—(except some ancient tricks),
New white-sticks, gold-sticks, broom-sticks, all new sticks !
With vests or ribands—deck'd alike in hue,
New troopers strut, new turncoats blush in blue :
So saith the muse : my ——[1], what say you ?
Such was the time when Waltz might best maintain
Her new preferments in this novel reign ;
Such was the time, nor ever yet was such ;
Hoops are *no more*, and petticoats *not much* ;
Morals and minuets, virtue and her stays,
And tell-tale powder—all have had their days.
The ball begins—the honours of the house
First duly done by daughter or by spouse,
Some potentate—or royal or serene—
With Kent's gay grace, or sapient Gloster's mien
Leads forth the ready dame, whose rising flush
Might once have been mistaken for a blush.
From where the garb just leaves the bosom free,
That spot where hearts were once supposed to be ;
Round all the confines of the yielded waist,
The strangest hand may wander undisplaced ;
The lady's in return may grasp as much
As princely paunches offer to her touch.
Pleased round the chalky floor how well they trip,
One hand reposing on the royal hip ;
The other to the shoulder no less royal,
Ascending with affection truly loyal !

[1] Here read ' Regent '—R.F.

47

Thus front to front the partners move or stand,
The foot may rest, but none withdraw the hand ;
And all in turn may follow in their rank,
The Earl of—Asterisk—and Lady—Blank ;
Sir—Such-a-one—with those of fashion's host,
For whose blest surnames—vide 'Morning Post.'
(Or if for that impartial print too late,
Search Doctors' Commons six months from my date)—
Thus all and each, in movement swift or slow,
The genial contact gently undergo ;
Till some might marvel, with the modest Turk
If 'nothing follows all this palming work ?'
True, honest Mirza !—you may trust my rhyme—
Something does follow at a fitter time ;
The breast thus publicly resign'd to man,
In private may resist him—if it can.

*

SONG FOR THE LUDDITES

I

As the Liberty lads o'er the sea
Bought their freedom, and cheaply, with blood,
    So we, boys, we
    Will *die* fighting, or *live* free,
And down with all kings but King Ludd !

II

When the web that we weave is complete,
And the shuttle exchanged for the sword,
    We will fling the winding sheet
    O'er the despot at our feet,
And dye it deep in the gore he has pour'd.

III

Though black as his heart its hue,
Since his veins are corrupted to mud,
    Yet this is the dew
    Which the tree shall renew
Of Liberty, planted by Ludd !

STANZAS

WHEN a man hath no freedom to fight for at home,
    Let him combat for that of his neighbours ;
Let him think of the glories of Greece and of Rome,
    And get knock'd on the head for his labours.

To do good to mankind is the chivalrous plan,
    And is always as nobly requited ;
Then battle for freedom wherever you can,
    And, if not shot or hang'd, you 'll get knighted.

TWO EPIGRAMS

THE world is a bundle of hay,
    Mankind are the asses who pull ;
Each tugs it a different way,
    And the greatest of all is John Bull.

So Castlereagh has cut his throat !—The worst
Of this, is—that his own was not the first.

TWO EPITAPHS

WILLIAM PITT

WITH death doom'd to grapple,
    Beneath this cold slab, he
Who lied in the Chapel
    Now lies in the Abbey.

LORD CASTLEREAGH

POSTERITY will ne'er survey
    A nobler grave than this :
Here lie the bones of Castlereagh :
    Stop, traveller ——

WINDSOR POETICS

Lines composed on the occasion of His Royal Highness the Prince Re
    being seen standing between the coffins of Henry VIII. and Charle
    in the royal vault at Windsor.

FAMED for contemptuous breach of sacred ties,
By headless Charles see heartless Henry lies ;
Between them stands another sceptred thing—
It moves, it reigns—in all but name, a king :

Charles to his people, Henry to his wife,
—In him the double tyrant starts to life :
Justice and death have mix'd their dust in vain,
Each royal vampire wakes to life again.
Ah, what can tombs avail !—since these disgorge
The blood and dust of both—to mould a George.

JOHN KEATS

WHO kill'd John Keats ?
    ' I,' says the Quarterly,
So savage and Tartarly ;
    ' 'T was one of my feats.'

Who shot the arrow ?
    ' The poet-priest Milman
(So ready to kill man),
    Or Southey, or Barrow.'

EPISTLE FROM MR. MURRAY TO DR. POLIDORI

DEAR Doctor, I have read your play,
Which is a good one in its way,—
Purges the eyes and moves the bowels,
And drenches handkerchiefs like towels
With tears, that, in a flux of grief,
Afford hysterical relief
To shatter'd nerves and quicken'd pulses,
Which your catastrophe convulses.

I like your moral and machinery ;
Your plot, too, has such scope for scenery ;
Your dialogue is apt and smart :
The play's concoction full of art ;
Your hero raves, your heroine cries,
All stab, and everybody dies.
In short, your tragedy would be
The very thing to hear and see :
And for a piece of publication,
If I decline on this occasion,
It is not that I am not sensible
To merits in themselves ostensible,
But—and I grieve to speak it—plays
Are drugs—mere drugs, sir—now-a-days.
I had a heavy loss by 'Manuel,'—
Too lucky if it prove not annual,—
And Sotheby, with his 'Orestes,'
(Which, by the by, the author's best is,)
Has lain so very long on hand,
That I despair of all demand.
I 've advertised, but see my books,
Or only watch my shopman's looks ;—
Still Ivan, Ina, and such lumber,
My back-shop glut, my shelves encumber,

There 's Byron too, who once did better,
Has sent me, folded in a letter,
A sort of—it 's no more a drama
Than Darnley, Ivan, or Kehama :
So alter'd since last year his pen is,
I think he 's lost his wits at Venice.
In short, sir, what with one and t' other,
I dare not venture on another.

I write in haste ; excuse each blunder ;
The coaches through the street so thunder !
My room 's so full—we 've Gifford here.
Reading MS., with Hookham Frere,
Pronouncing on the nouns and particles
Of some of our forthcoming Articles.

The Quarterly—Ah, sir, if you
Had but the genius to review !—
A smart critique upon St. Helena,
Or if you only would but tell in a
Short compass what——but to resume :
As I was saying, sir, the room—
The room 's so full of wits and bards,
Crabbes, Campbells, Crokers, Freres, and Wards,
And others, neither bards nor wits :—
My humble tenement admits
All persons in the dress of gent,
From Mr. Hammond to Dog Dent.

A party dines with me to-day,
All clever men, who make their way.
Crabbe, Malcolm, Hamilton, and Chantrey,
Are all partakers of my pantry.
They're at this moment in discussion
On poor De Staël's late dissolution.
Her book, they say, was in advance—
Pray Heaven, she tell the truth of France !
Thus run our time and tongues away ;—
But, to return, sir, to your play.
Sorry, sir, but I cannot deal,
Unless 't were acted by O'Neill ;
My hands so full, my head so busy,
I 'm almost dead, and always dizzy ;
And so, with endless truth and hurry,
Dear Doctor, I am yours,

JOHN MURRAY.

THE VISION OF JUDGMENT

I

SAINT PETER sat by the celestial gate :
   His keys were rusty, and the lock was dull,
So little trouble had been given of late ;
   Not that the place by any means was full,
But since the Gallic era 'eighty-eight'
   The devils had ta'en a longer, stronger pull,
And 'a pull altogether,' as they say
At sea—which drew most souls another way.

II

The angels all were singing out of tune,
   And hoarse with having little else to do,
Excepting to wind up the sun and moon,
   Or curb a runaway young star or two,
Or wild colt of a comet, which too soon
   Broke out of bounds o'er th' ethereal blue,
Splitting some planet with its playful tail,
As boats are sometimes by a wanton whale.

III

The guardian seraphs had retired on high,
   Finding their charges past all care below ;
Terrestrial business fill'd nought in the sky
   Save the recording angel's black bureau ;
Who found, indeed, the facts to multiply
   With such rapidity of vice and woe,
That he had stripp'd off both his wings in quills,
And yet was in arrear of human ills.

IV

His business so augmented of late years,
   That he was forced, against his will no doubt,
(Just like those cherubs, earthly ministers,)
   For some resource to turn himself about,
And claim the help of his celestial peers,
   To aid him ere he should be quite worn out
By the increased demand for his remarks :
Six angels and twelve saints were named his clerks.

V

This was a handsome board—at least for heaven ;
   And yet they had even then enough to do,
So many conquerors' cars were daily driven,
   So many kingdoms fitted up anew ;

Each day too slew its thousands six or seven,
  Till at the crowning carnage, Waterloo,
They threw their pens down in divine disgust—
The page was so besmear'd with blood and dust.

VI

This by the way ; 't is not mine to record
  What angels shrink from : even the very devil
On this occasion his own work abhorr'd,
  So surfeited with the infernal revel :
Though he himself had sharpen'd every sword,
  It almost quench'd his innate thirst of evil.
(Here Satan's sole good work deserves insertion—
'T is, that he has both generals in reversion.)

VII

Let's skip a few short years of hollow peace,
  Which peopled earth no better, hell as wont,
And heaven none—they form the tyrant's lease,
  With nothing but new names subscribed upon't ;
'T will one day finish : meantime they increase,
  ' With seven heads and ten horns,' and all in front,
Like Saint John's foretold beast ; but ours are born
Less formidable in the head than horn.

VIII

In the first year of freedom's second dawn
  Died George the Third ; although no tyrant, one
Who shielded tyrants, till each sense withdrawn
  Left him nor mental nor external sun :
A better farmer ne'er brush'd dew from lawn,
  A weaker king ne'er left a realm undone !
He died—but left his subjects still behind
One half as mad—and t' other no less blind.

IX

He died ! his death made no great stir on earth :
  His burial made some pomp ; there was profusion
Of velvet, gilding, brass, and no great dearth
  Of aught but tears—save those shed by collusion.
For these things may be bought at their true worth ;
  Of elegy there was the due infusion—
Bought also ; and the torches, cloaks, and banners,
Heralds, and relics of old Gothic manners,

Form'd a sepulchral melodrame.   Of all
 The fools who flock'd to swell or see the show,
Who cared about the corpse ?   The funeral
 Made the attraction, and the black the woe.
There throbb'd not there a thought which pierced the pall;
 And when the gorgeous coffin was laid low,
It seem'd the mockery of hell to fold
The rottenness of eighty years in gold.

XI

So mix his body with the dust !   It might
 Return to what it *must* far sooner, were
The natural compound left alone to fight
 Its way back into earth, and fire, and air ;
But the unnatural balsams merely blight
 What nature made him at his birth, as bare
As the mere million's base unmummied clay—
Yet all his spices but prolong decay.

XII

He's dead—and upper earth with him has done ;
 He's buried ; save the undertaker's bill,
Or lapidary scrawl, the world is gone
 For him, unless he left a German will :
But where's the proctor who will ask his son ?
 In whom his qualities are reigning still,
Except that household virtue, most uncommon,
Of constancy to an unhandsome woman.

XIII

'God save the king !'   It is a large economy
 In God to save the like ; but if he will
Be saving, all the better ; for not one am I
 Of those who think damnation better still :
I hardly know too if not quite alone am I
 In this small hope of bettering future ill
By circumscribing, with some slight restriction,
The eternity of hell's hot jurisdiction.

XIV

I know this is unpopular ; I know
 'T is blasphemous ; I know one may be damn'd
For hoping no one else may e'er be so :
 I know my catechism ; I know we're cramm'd

55

With the best doctrines till we quite o'erflow ;
 I know that all save England's church have shamm'd,
And that the other twice two hundred churches
And synagogues have made a *damn'd* bad purchase.

XV

God help us all ! God help me too ! I am,
 God knows, as helpless as the devil can wish,
And not a whit more difficult to damn,
 Than is to bring to land a late-hook'd fish,
Or to the butcher to purvey the lamb ;
 Not that I'm fit for such a noble dish,
As one day will be that immortal fry
Of almost everybody born to die.

XVI

Saint Peter sat by the celestial gate,
 And nodded o'er his keys ; when, lo ! there came
A wondrous noise he had not heard of late—
 A rushing sound of wind, and stream, and flame ;
In short, a roar of things extremely great,
 Which would have made aught save a saint exclaim ;
But he, with first a start and then a wink,
Said, ' There's another star gone out, I think ! '

XVII

But ere he could return to his repose,
 A cherub flapp'd his right wing o'er his eyes—
At which St. Peter yawn'd, and rubb'd his nose ;
 ' Saint porter,' said the angel, ' prithee rise ! '
Waving a goodly wing, which glow'd as glows
 An earthly peacock's tail, with heavenly dyes :
To which the saint replied, ' Well what's the matter ?
Is Lucifer come back with all this clatter ? '

XVIII

' No,' quoth the cherub ; ' George the Third is dead.'
 ' And who *is* George the Third ? ' replied the apostle :
' *What George ? what Third ?* ' ' The king of England,' sa
 The angel. ' Well ! he won't find kings to jostle
Him on his way ; but does he wear his head ?
 Because the last we had here had a tustle,
And ne'er would have got into heaven's good graces,
Had he not flung his head in all our faces.

XIX

' He was, if I remember, king of France ;
 That head of his, which could not keep a crown
On earth, yet ventured in my face to advance
 A claim to those of martyrs—like my own ;
If I had had my sword, as I had once
 When I cut ears off, I had cut him down ;
But having but my *keys*, and not my brand,
I only knock'd his head from out his hand.

XX

' And then he set up such a headless howl,
 That all the saints came out and took him in ;
And there he sits by St. Paul, cheek by jowl ;
 That fellow Paul—the parvenu ! The skin
Of St. Bartholomew, which makes his cowl
 In heaven, and upon earth redeem'd his sin,
So as to make a martyr, never sped
Better than did this weak and wooden head.

XXI

' But had it come up here upon its shoulders,
 There would have been a different tale to tell
The fellow-feeling in the saints beholders
 Seems to have acted on them like a spell ;
And so this very foolish head heaven solder
 Back on its trunk : it may be very well,
And seems the custom here to overthrow
Whatever has been wisely done below.'

XXII

The angel answer'd, ' Peter ! do not pout :
 The king who comes has head and all entire,
And never knew much what it was about—
 He did as doth the puppet—by its wire,
And will be judged like all the rest no doubt :
 My business and your own is not to inquire
Into such matters, but to mind our cue—
Which is to act as we are bid to do.'

XXIII

While thus they spake, the angelic caravan,
 Arriving like a rush of mighty wind,
Cleaving the fields of space, as doth the swan
 Some silver stream (say Ganges, Nile, or Inde,

Or Thames, or Tweed), and 'midst them an old man
  With an old soul, and both extremely blind.
Halted before the gate, and in his shroud
Seated their fellow traveller on a cloud.

XXIV

But bringing up the rear of this bright host
  A spirit of a different aspect waved
His wings, like thunder-clouds above some coast
  Whose barren beach with frequent wrecks is paved ;
His brow was like the deep when tempest-toss'd ;
  Fierce and unfathomable thoughts engraved
Eternal wrath on his immortal face,
And *where* he gazed a gloom pervaded space.

XXV

As he drew near, he gazed upon the gate
  Ne'er to be enter'd more by him or Sin,
With such a glance of supernatural hate,
  As made Saint Peter wish himself within ;
He patter'd with his keys at a great rate,
  And sweated through his apostolic skin :
Of course his perspiration was but ichor,
Or some such other spiritual liquor.

XXVI

The very cherubs huddled all together,
  Like birds when soars the falcon ; and they felt
A tingling to the tip of every feather,
  And form'd a circle like Orion's belt
Around their poor old charge ; who scarce knew whither
  His guards had led him, though they gently dealt
With royal manes (for by many stories,
And true, we learn the angels all are Tories).

XXVII

As things were in this posture, the gate flew
  Asunder, and the flashing of its hinges
Flung over space an universal hue
  Of many-colour'd flame, until its tinges
Reach'd even our speck of earth, and made a new
  Aurora borealis spread its fringes
O'er the North Pole ; the same seen, when ice-bound,
By Captain Parry's crew, in 'Melville's Sound.'

XXVIII

And from the gate thrown open issued beaming
  A beautiful and mighty Thing of Light,
Radiant with glory, like a banner streaming
  Victorious from some world-o'erthrowing fight :
My poor comparisons must needs be teeming
  With earthly likenesses, for here the night
Of clay obscures our best conceptions, saving
Johanna Southcote, or Bob Southey raving.

XXIX

'T was the archangel Michael ; all men know
  The make of angels and archangels, since
There's scarce a scribbler has not one to show,
  From the fiends' leader to the angels' prince ;
There also are some altar-pieces, though
  I really can 't say that they much evince
One's inner notions of immortal spirits ;
But let the connoisseurs explain *their* merits.

XXX

Michael flew forth in glory and in good ;
  A goodly work of him from whom all glory
And good arise ; the portal past—he stood ;
  Before him the young cherubs and saints hoary—
(I say *young*, begging to be understood
  By looks, not years ; and should be very sorry
To state, they were not older than St. Peter,
But merely that they seem'd a little sweeter).

XXXI

The cherubs and the saints bow'd down before
  That arch-angelic hierarch, the first
Of essences angelical, who wore
  The aspect of a god ; but this ne'er nursed
Pride in his heavenly bosom, in whose core
  No thought, save for his Master's service, durst
Intrude, however glorified and high ;
He knew him but the viceroy of the sky.

XXXII

He and the sombre, silent Spirit met—
  They knew each other both for good and ill ;
Such was their power, that neither could forget
  His former friend and future foe ; but still

59

There was a high immortal proud regret
   In either's eye, as if 't were less their will
Than destiny to make the eternal years
Their date of war, and their 'champ clos' the spheres.

XXXIII

But here they were in neutral space : we know
   From Job, that Satan hath the power to pay
A heavenly visit thrice a year or so ;
   And that the 'sons of God,' like those of clay,
Must keep him company ; ; and we might show
   From the same book, in how polite a way
The dialogue is held between the Powers
Of Good and Evil—but 't would take up hours.

XXXIV

And this is not a theologic tract,
   To prove with Hebrew and with Arabic,
If Job be allegory or a fact,
   But a true narrative ; and thus I pick
From out the whole but such and such an act
   As sets aside the slightest thought of trick.
'T is every tittle true, beyond suspicion,
And accurate as any other vision.

XXXV

The spirits were in neutral space, before
   The gate of heaven ; like eastern thresholds is
The place where Death's grand cause is argued o'er,
   And souls despatch'd to that world or to this ;
And therefore Michael and the other wore
   A civil aspect : though they did not kiss,
Yet still between his Darkness and his Brightness
There passed a mutual glance of great politeness.

XXXVI

The Archangel bow'd, not like a modern beau,
   But with a graceful Oriental bend
Pressing one radiant arm just where below
   The heart of good men is supposed to tend ;
He turn'd as to an equal, not too low,
   But kindly ; Satan met his ancient friend
With more hauteur, as might an old Castilian
Poor noble meet a mushroom rich civilian.

XXXVII

He merely bent his diabolic brow
   An instant ; and then raising it, he stood
In act to assert his right or wrong, and show
   Cause why King George by no means could or should
Make out a case to be exempt from woe
   Eternal, more than other kings, endued
With better sense and hearts, whom history mentions,
Who long have ' paved hell with their good intentions.'

XXXVIII

Michael began : ' What wouldst thou with this man,
   Now dead, and brought before the Lord ? What ill
Hath he wrought since his mortal race began,
   That thou canst claim him ? Speak ! and do thy will,
If it be just : if in this earthly span
   He hath been greatly failing to fulfil
His duties as a king and mortal, say
And he is thine ; if not, let him have way.'

XXXIX

' Michael ! ' replied the Prince of Air, ' even here
   Before the Gate of him thou servest, must
I claim my subject : and will make appear
   That as he was my worshipper in dust,
So shall he be in spirit, although dear
   To thee and thine, because nor wine nor lust
Were of his weaknesses ; yet on the throne
He reign'd o'er millions to serve me alone.

XL

' Look to *our* earth, or rather *mine* ; it was,
   Once, *more* thy master's : but I triumph not
In this poor planet's conquest ; nor, alas !
   Need he thou servest envy me my lot :
With all the myriads of bright worlds which pass
   In worship round him, he may have forgot
Yon weak creation of such paltry things :
I think few worth damnation save their kings,—

XLI

And these but as a kind of quit-rent, to
   Assert my right as lord : and even had
I such an inclination, 't were (as you
   Well know) superfluous ; they are grown so bad,

That hell has nothing better left to do
    Than leave them to themselves : so much more mad
And evil by their own internal curse,
Heaven cannot make them better, nor I worse.

XLII

' Look to the earth, I said, and say again :
    When this old, blind, mad, helpless, weak, poor worm
Began in youth's first bloom and flush to reign,
    The world and he both wore a different form,
And much of earth and all the watery plain
    Of ocean call'd him king : through many a storm
His isles had floated on the abyss of time ;
For the rough virtues chose them for their clime.

XLIII

' He came to his sceptre young ; he leaves it old :
    Look to the state in which he found his realm,
And left it ; and his annals too behold,
    How to a minion first he gave the helm ;
How grew upon his heart a thirst for gold,
    The beggar's vice, which can but overwhelm
The meanest hearts ; and for the rest, but glance
Thine eye along America and France.

XLIV

' 'T is true, he was a tool from first to last
    (I have the workmen safe) ; but as a tool
So let him be consumed.   From out the past
    Of ages, since mankind have known the rule
Of monarchs—from the bloody rolls amass'd
    Of sin and slaughter—from the Cæsar's school,
Take the worst pupil ; and produce a reign
More drench'd with gore, more cumber'd with the slain.

XLV

' He ever warr'd with freedom and the free :
    Nations as men, home subjects, foreign foes,
So that they utter'd the word " Liberty ! "
    Found George the Third their first opponent.   Whose
History was ever stain'd as his will be
    With national and individual woes ?
I grant his household abstinence ; I grant
His neutral virtues, which most monarchs want :

' I know he was a constant consort ; own
  He was a decent sire, and middling lord.
All this is much, and most upon a throne ;
  As temperance, if at Apicius' board,
Is more than at an anchorite's supper shown.
  I grant him all the kindest can accord ;
And this was well for him, but not for those
Millions who found him what oppression chose.

XLVII

' The New World shook him off ; the Old yet groans
  Beneath what he and his prepared, if not
Completed : he leaves heirs on many thrones
  To all his vices, without what begot
Compassion for him—his tame virtues ; drones
  Who sleep, or despots who have now forgot
A lesson which shall be re-taught them, wake
Upon the thrones of earth ; but let them quake !

XLVIII

' Five millions of the primitive, who hold
  The faith which makes ye great on earth, implored
A *part* of that vast *all* they held of old,—
  Freedom to worship—not alone your Lord,
Michael, but you, and you, Saint Peter ! Cold
  Must be your souls, if you have not abhorr'd
The foe to Catholic participation
In all the license of a Christian nation.

XLIX

' True ! he allow'd them to pray God ; but as
  A consequence of prayer, refused the law
Which would have placed them upon the same base
  With those who did not hold the saints in awe.'
But here Saint Peter started from his place,
  And cried, ' You may the prisoner withdraw :
Ere heaven shall ope her portals to this Guelph.
While I am guard, may I be damn'd myself !

L

' Sooner will I with Cerberus exchange
  My office (and *his* is no sinecure)
Than see this royal Bedlam bigot range
  The azure fields of heaven, of that be sure !'

'Saint!' replied Satan, 'you do well to avenge
   The wrongs he made your satellites endure ;
And if to this exchange you should be given,
I'll try to coax *our* Cerberus up to heaven!'

LI

Here Michael interposed : ' Good saint! and devil!
   Pray, not so fast ; you both outrun discretion.
Saint Peter! you were wont to be more civil!
   Satan! excuse this warmth of his expression,
And condescension to the vulgar's level :
   Even saints sometimes forget themselves in session.
Have you got more to say ?'—' No.'—' If you please,
I'll trouble you to call your witnesses.'

LII

Then Satan turn'd and waved his swarthy hand,
   Which stirr'd with its electric qualities
Clouds farther off than we can understand,
   Although we find him sometimes in our skies ;
Infernal thunder shook both sea and land
   In all the planets, and hell's batteries
Let off the artillery, which Milton mentions
As one of Satan's most sublime inventions.

LIII

This was a signal unto such damn'd souls
   As have the privilege of their damnation
Extended far beyond the mere controls
   Of worlds past, present, or to come ; no station
Is theirs particularly in the rolls
   Of hell assign'd ; but where their inclination
Or business carries them in search of game,
They may range freely—being damn'd the same.

LIV

They're proud of this—as very well they may,
   It being a sort of knighthood, or gilt key
Stuck in their loins ; or like to an ' entré '
   Up the back stairs, or such free-masonry.
I borrow my comparisons from clay,
   Being clay myself. Let not those spirits be
Offended with such base low likenesses ;
We know their posts are nobler far than these.

When the great signal ran from heaven to hell—
   About ten million times the distance reckon'd
From our sun to its earth, as we can tell
   How much time it takes up, even to a second,
For every ray that travels to dispel
   The fogs of London, through which, dimly beacon'd,
The weathercocks are gilt some thrice a year,
If that the *summer* is not too severe :

I say that I can tell—'t was half a minute ;
   I know the solar beams take up more time
Ere, pack'd up for their journey, they begin it ;
   But then their telegraph is less sublime,
And if they ran a race, they would not win it
   'Gainst Satan's couriers bound for their own clime.
The sun takes up some years for every ray
To reach its goal—the devil not half a day.

Upon the verge of space, about the size
   Of half-a-crown, a little speck appear'd
(I've seen a something like it in the skies
   In the Ægean, ere a squall) ; it near'd,
And, growing bigger, took another guise ;
   Like an aërial ship it tack'd, and steer'd,
Or *was* steer'd (I am doubtful of the grammar
Of the last phrase, which makes the stanza stammer ;—

But take your choice) : and then it grew a cloud ;
   And so it was—a cloud of witnesses.
But such a cloud ! No land e'er saw a crowd
   Of locusts numerous as the heavens saw these ;
They shadow'd with their myriads space ; their loud
   And varied cries were like those of wild geese
(If nations may be liken'd to a goose),
And realised the phrase of ' hell broke loose.'

Here crash'd a sturdy oath of stout John Bull,
   Who damn'd away his eyes as heretofore :
There Paddy brogued ' By Jasus ! '—' What's your wull ? '
   The temperate Scot exclaim'd : the French ghost swore

In certain terms I shan't translate in full,
    As the first coachman will ; and 'midst the roar,
The voice of Jonathan was heard to express,
' *Our* president is going to war, I guess.'

LX

Besides there were the Spaniard, Dutch, and Dane ;
    In short, an universal shoal of shades,
From Otaheite's isle to Salisbury Plain,
    Of all climes and professions, years and trades,
Ready to swear against the good king's reign,
    Bitter as clubs in cards are against spades :
All summon'd by this grand ' subpœna,' to
Try if kings mayn't be damn'd like me or you.

LXI

When Michael saw this host, he first grew pale,
    As angels can ; next, like Italian twilight,
He turn'd all colours—as a peacock's tail,
    Or sunset streaming through a Gothic skylight
In some old abbey, or a trout not stale,
    Or distant lightning on the horizon *by* night,
Or a fresh rainbow, or a grand review
Of thirty regiments in red, green, and b ue.

LXII

Then he address'd himself to Satan : ' Why—
    My good old friend, for such I deem you, though
Our different parties make us fight so shy ;
    I ne'er mistake you for a *personal* foe ;
Our difference is *political*, and I
    Trust that, whatever may occur below,
You know my great respect for you : and this
Makes me regret what'er you do amiss—

LXIII

' Why, my dear Lucifer, would you abuse
    My call for witnesses ? I did not mean
That you should half of earth and hell produce ;
    'T is even superfluous, since two honest, clean,
True testimonies are enough : we lose
    Our time, nay, our eternity, between
The accusation and defence : if we
Hear both, 't will stretch our immortality.'

LXIV

Satan replied, ' To me the matter is
　　Indifferent, in a personal point of view :
I can have fifty better souls than this
　　With far less trouble than we have gone through
Already ; and I merely argued his
　　Late majesty of Britain's case with you
Upon a point of form : you may dispose
Of him ; I 've kings enough below, God knows !'

LXV

Thus spoke the Demon (late call'd ' multifaced '
　　By multo-scribbling Southey). ' Then we'll call
One or two persons of the myriads placed
　　Around our congress, and dispense with all
The rest,' quoth Michael : ' Who may be so graced
　　As to speak first ? there's choice enough—who shall
It be ? ' Then Satan answer'd, ' There are many ;
But you may choose Jack Wilkes as well as any.'

LXVI

A merry, cock-eyed, curious-looking sprite
　　Upon the instant started from the throng,
Dress'd in a fashion now forgotten quite ;
　　For all the fashions of the flesh stick long
By people in the next world ; where unite
　　All the costumes since Adam's, right or wrong,
From Eve's fig-leaf down to the petticoat,
Almost as scanty, of days less remote.

LXVII

The spirit look'd around upon the crowds
　　Assembled, and exclaim'd, ' My friends of all
The spheres, we shall catch cold amongst these clouds
　　So let's to business : why this general call ?
If those are freeholders I see in shrouds,
　　And 't is for an election that they bawl,
Behold a candidate with unturn'd coat !
Saint Peter, may I count upon your vote ? '

LXVIII

' Sir,' replied Michael, ' you mistake ; these things
　　Are of a former life, and what we do
Above is more august ; to judge of kings
　　Is the tribunal met : so now you know.'

' Then I presume those gentlemen with wings,'
 Said Wilkes, ' are cherubs ; and that soul below
Looks much like George the Third, but to my mind
A good deal older—Bless me ! is he blind ? '

LXIX

' He is what you behold him, and his doom
 Depends upon his deeds,' the Angel said ;
' If you have aught to arraign in him, the tomb
 Gives license to the humblest beggar's head
To lift itself against the loftiest.'—' Some,'
 Said Wilkes, ' don't wait to see them laid in lead,
For such a liberty—and I, for one,
Have told them what I thought beneath the sun.'

LXX

' *Above* the sun repeat, then, what thou hast
 To urge against him,' said the Archangel. ' Why,'
Replied the spirit, ' since old scores are past,
 Must I turn evidence ?   In faith, not I.
Besides, I beat him hollow at the last,
 With all his Lords and Commons : in the sky
I don't like ripping up old stories, since
His conduct was but natural in a prince.

LXXI

' Foolish, no doubt, and wicked, to oppress
 A poor unlucky devil without a shilling ;
But then I blame the man himself much less
 Than Bute and Grafton, and shall be unwilling
To see him punish'd here for their excess,
 Since they were both damn'd long ago, and still in
Their place below : for me, I have forgiven,
And vote his " habeas corpus " into heaven.'

LXXII

' Wilkes,' said the Devil, ' I understand all this
 You turn'd to half a courtier ere you died,
And seem to think it would not be amiss
 To grow a whole one on the other side
Of Charon's ferry ; you forget that *his*
 Reign is concluded ; whatsoe'er betide
He won't be sovereign more : you've lost your labour
For at the best he will but be your neighbour.

68

'However, I knew what to think of it,
  When I beheld you in your jesting way,
Flitting and whispering round about the spit
  Where Belial upon duty for the day,
With Fox's lard was basting William Pitt,
  His pupil ; I knew what to think, I say
That fellow even in hell breeds farther ills ;
I 'll have him *gagg'd*—'t was one of his own bills.

LXXIV

' Call Junius !' From the crowd a shadow stalk'd,
  And at the name there was a general squeeze,
So that the very ghosts no longer walk'd
  In comfort, at their own aërial ease,
But were all ramm'd, and jamm'd (but to be balk'd,
  As we shall see), and jostled hands and knees,
Like wind compress'd and pent within a bladder,
Or like a human colic, which is sadder.

LXXV

The shadow came—a tall, thin, grey-hair'd figure,
  That look'd as it had been a shade on earth ;
Quick in its motions, with an air of vigour,
  But nought to mark its breeding or its birth ;
Now it wax'd little, then again grew bigger,
  With now an air of gloom, or savage mirth ;
But as you gazed upon its features they
Changed every instant—to *what*, none could say.

LXXVI

The more intently the ghosts gazed, the less
  Could they distinguish whose the features were ;
The Devil himself seem'd puzzled even to guess ;
  They varied like a dream—now here, now there
And several people swore from out the press,
  They knew him perfectly ; and one could swear
He was his father ; upon which another
Was sure he was his mother's cousin's brother :

LXXVII

Another, that he was a duke, or knight,
  An orator, a lawyer, or a priest,
A nabob, a man-midwife ; but the wight
  Mysterious changed his countenance at least

As oft as they their minds ; though in full sight
　　He stood, the puzzle only was increased ;
The man was a phantasmagoria in
Himself—he was so volatile and thin.

LXXVIII

The moment you had pronounced him *one*,
　　Presto ! his face changed, and he was another ;
And when that change was hardly well put on,
　　It varied, till I don't think his own mother
(If that he had a mother) would her son
　　Have known, he shifted so from one to t' other ;
Till guessing from a pleasure grew a task,
At this epistolary ' Iron Mask.'

LXXIX

For sometimes he like Cerberus would seem—
　　' Three gentlemen at once ' (as sagely says
Good Mrs. Malaprop) ; then you might deem
　　That he was not even *one ;* now many rays
Were flashing round him ; and now a thick steam
　　Hid him from sight—like fogs on London days :
Now Burke, now Tooke, he grew to people's fancies,
And certes often like Sir Philip Francis.

LXXX

I've an hypothesis—'t is quite my own ;
　　I never let it out till now, for fear
Of doing people harm about the throne,
　　And injuring some minister or peer,
On whom the stigma might perhaps be blown ;
　　It is—my gentle public, lend thine ear !
'T is, that what Junius we are wont to call
Was *really*, *truly*, nobody at all.

LXXXI

I don't see wherefore letters should not be
　　Written without hands, since we daily view
Them written without heads ; and books, we see
　　Are fill'd as well without the latter too :
And really till we fix on somebody
　　For certain sure to claim them as his due,
Their author, like the Niger's mouth, will bother
The world to say if *there* be mouth or author.

LXXXII

And who and what art thou ?' the Archangel said.
  'For *that* you may consult my title-page,'
Replied this mighty shadow of a shade :
  'If I have kept my secret half an age,
I scarce shall tell it now.'—' Canst thou upbraid,'
  Continued Michael, ' George Rex, or allege
Aught further ?' Junius answer'd, ' You had better
First ask him for *his* answer to my letter :

LXXXIII

My charges upon record will outlast
  The brass of both his epitaph and tomb.'
Repent'st thou not,' said Michael, ' of some past
  Exaggeration ? something which may doom
Thyself if false, as him if true ? Thou wast
  Too bitter—is it not so ?—in thy gloom
Of passion ?'—' Passion ! ' cried the phantom dim,
' I loved my country, and I hated him.

LXXXIV

' What I have written, I have written : let
  The rest be on his head or mine ! ' So spoke
Old ' Nominis Umbra ; ' and while speaking yet,
  Away he melted in celestial smoke.
Then Satan said to Michael, ' Don't forget
  To call George Washington, and John Horne Tooke,
And Franklin ; '—but at this time there was heard
A cry for room, though not a phantom stirr'd.

LXXXV

At length with jostling, elbowing, and the aid
  Of cherubim appointed to that post,
The devil Asmodeus to the circle made
  His way, and look'd as if his journey cost
Some trouble. When his burden down he laid,
  'What's this ?' cried Michael ; ' why, 't is not a ghost ?'
' I know it,' quoth the incubus ; ' but he
Shall be one, if you leave the affair to me.

LXXXVI

' Confound the renegado ! I have sprain'd
  My left wing, he's so heavy ; one would think
Some of his works about his neck were chain'd.
  But to the point ; while hovering o'er the brink

71

Of Skiddaw (where as usual it still rain'd),
     I saw a taper, far below me wink,
And stooping, caught this fellow at a libel—
No less on history than the Holy Bible.

LXXXVII

' The former is the devil's scripture, and
     The latter yours, good Michael : so the affair
Belongs to all of us, you understand.
     I snatch'd him up just as you see him there,
And brought him off for sentence out of hand :
     I've scarcely been ten minutes in the air—
At least a quarter it can hardly be :
I dare say that his wife is still at tea.'

LXXXVIII

Here Satan said, ' I know this man of old,
     And have expected him for some time here ;
A sillier fellow you will scarce behold,
     Or more conceited in his petty sphere :
But surely it was not worth while to fold
     Such trash below your wing, Asmodeus dear :
We had the poor wretch safe (without being bored
With carriage) coming of his own accord.

LXXXIX

' But since he's here, let's see what he has done.'
     ' Done ! ' cried Asmodeus, ' he anticipates
The very business you are now upon,
     And scribbles as if head clerk to the Fates.
Who knows to what his ribaldry may run,
     When such an ass as this, like Balaam's prates ? '
' Let's hear,' quoth Michael, ' what he has to say :
You know we're bound to that in every way.'

XC

Now the bard, glad to get an audience, which
     By no means often was his case below,
Began to cough, and hawk, and hem, and pitch
     His voice into that awful note of woe
To all unhappy hearers within reach
     Of poets when the tide of rhyme's in flow ;
But stuck fast with his first hexameter,
Not one of all whose gouty feet would stir.

But ere the spavin'd dactyls could be spurr'd
   Into recitative, in great dismay
Both cherubim and seraphim were heard
   To murmur loudly through their long array ;
And Michael rose ere he could get a word
   Of all his founder'd verses under way,
And cried, ' For God's sake stop, my friend ! 'twere best—
Non Di, non homines—you know the rest.'

A general bustle spread throughout the throng,
   Which seem'd to hold all verse in detestation ;
The angels had of course enough of song
   When upon service ; and the generation
Of ghosts had heard too much in life, not long
   Before, to profit by a new occasion :
The monarch, mute till then, exclaim'd, ' What ! what !
Pye come again. No more—no more of that ! '

The tumult grew ; an universal cough
   Convulsed the skies, as during a debate,
When Castlereagh has been up long enough
   (Before he was first minister of state,
I mean—the *slaves hear now*) ; some cried ' Off, off ! '
   As at a farce ; till, grown quite desperate,
The bard·Saint Peter pray'd to interpose
(Himself an author) only for his prose.

The varlet was not an ill-favour'd knave ;
   A good deal like a vulture in the face,
With a hook nose and a hawk's eye, which gave
   A smart and sharper-looking sort of grace
To his whole aspect, which, though rather grave,
   Was by no means so ugly as his case ;
But that, indeed, was hopeless as can be,
Quite a poetic felony ' *de se.*'

Then Michael blew his trump, and still'd the noise
   With one still greater, as is yet the mode
On earth besides ; except some grumbling voice,
   Which now and then will make a slight inroad

Upon decorous silence, few will twice
    Lift up their lungs when fairly overcrow'd ;
And now the bard could plead his own bad cause,
With all the attitudes of self-applause.

XCVI

He said—(I only give the heads)—he said,
    He meant no harm in scribbling ; 't was his way
Upon all topics ; 't was, besides, his bread,
    Of which he butter'd both sides ; 't would delay
Too long the assembly (he was pleased to dread),
    And take up rather more time than a day,
To name his works—he would but cite a few—
' Wat Tyler '—' Rhymes on Blenheim '—' Waterloo.'

XCVII

He had written praises of a regicide ;
    He had written praises of all kings whatever ;
He had written for republics far and wide,
    And then against them bitterer than ever ;
For pantisocracy he once had cried
    Aloud, a scheme less moral than 't was clever ;
Then grew a hearty anti-jacobin—
Had turn'd his coat—and would have turn'd his skin.

XCVIII

He had sung against all battles, and again
    In their high praise and glory : he had call'd
Reviewing ' the ungentle craft,' and then
    Become as base a critic as e'er crawl'd—
Fed, paid, and pamper'd by the very men
    By whom his muse and morals had been maul'd
He had written much blank verse, and blanker prose,
And more of both than anybody knows.

XCIX

He had written Wesley's life :—here turning round
    To Satan, ' Sir, I'm ready to write yours,
In two octavo volumes, nicely bound,
    With notes and preface, all that most allures
The pious purchaser ; and there's no ground
    For fear, for I can choose my own reviewers :
So let me have the proper documents,
That I may add you to my other saints.'

Satan bow'd, and was silent. 'Well, if you,
   With amiable modesty, decline
My offer, what says Michael ? There are few
   Whose memoirs could be render'd more divine.
Mine is a pen of all work ; not so new
   As it was once, but I would make you shine
Like your own trumpet. By the way, my own
Has more of brass in it, and is as well blown.

CI

' But talking about trumpets, here 's my Vision !
   Now you shall judge, all people ; yes, you shall
Judge with my judgment, and by my decision
   Be guided who shall enter heaven or fall.
I settle all these things by intuition,
   Times present, past, to come, heaven, hell, and all,
Like King Alfonso. When I thus see double,
I save the Deity some worlds of trouble.'

CII

He ceased, and drew forth an MS. ; and no
   Persuasion on the part of devils, saints,
Or angels, now could stop the torrent ; so
   He read the first three lines of the contents ;
But at the fourth, the whole spiritual show
   Had vanish'd, with variety of scents,
Ambrosial and sulphureous, as they sprang,
Like lightning, off from his ' melodious twang.'

CIII

Those grand heroics acted as a spell :
   The angels stopp'd their ears and plied their pinions ;
The devils ran howling, deafen'd, down to hell ;
   The ghosts fled, gibbering, for their own dominions—
(For 't is not yet decided where they dwell,
   And I leave every man to his opinions) ;
Michael took refuge in his trump—but, lo !
His teeth were set on edge, he could not blow !

CIV

Saint Peter, who has hitherto been known
   For an impetuous saint, upraised his keys,
And at the fifth line knock'd the poet down ;
   Who fell like Phaeton, but more at ease,

Into his lake, for there he did not drown ;
　　A different web being by the Destinies
Woven for the Laureate's final wreath, whene'er
Reform shall happen either here or there.

CV

He first sank to the bottom—like his works,
　　But soon rose to the surface—like himself ;
For all corrupted things are buoy'd like corks,
　　By their own rottenness, light as an elf,
Or wisp that flits o'er a morass ; he lurks,
　　It may be, still, like dull books on a shelf,
In his own den, to scrawl some ' Life ' or ' Vision,'
As Welborn says—' the devil turn'd precisian.'

CVI

As for the rest, to come to the conclusion
　　Of this true dream, the telescope is gone
Which kept my optics free from all delusion,
　　And show'd me what I in my turn have shown ;
All I saw farther, in the last confusion,
　　Was that King George slipped into heaven for one ;
And when the tumult dwindled to a calm,
I left him practising the hundredth psalm.

FROM
DON JUAN

CANTO I

I

I WANT a hero : an uncommon want,
  When every year and month sends forth a new one,
Till, after cloying the gazettes with cant,
  The age discovers he is not the true one :
Of such as these I should not care to vaunt,
  I'll therefore take our ancient friend Don Juan—
We all have seen him, in the pantomime,
Sent to the devil somewhat ere his time.

II

Vernon, the butcher Cumberland, Wolfe, Hawke,
  Prince Ferdinand, Granby, Burgoyne, Keppel, Howe,
Evil and good, have had their tithe of talk,
  And fill'd their sign-posts then, like Wellesley now ;
Each in their turn like Banquo's monarchs stalk,
  Followers of fame, ' nine farrow ' of that sow :
France, too, had Buonaparté and Dumourier
Recorded in the Moniteur and Courier.

III

Barnave, Brissot, Condorcet, Mirabeau,
  Pétion, Clootz, Danton, Marat, La Fayette,
Were French, and famous people, as we know ;
  And there were others, scarce forgotten yet,
Joubert, Hoche, Marceau, Lannes, Desaix, Moreau,
  With many of the military set,
Exceedingly remarkable at times,
But not at all adapted to my rhymes.

IV

Nelson was once Britannia's god of war,
  And still should be so, but the tide is turn'd ;
There's no more to be said of Trafalgar,
  'T is with our hero quietly inurn'd ;
Because the army's grown more popular,
  At which the naval people are concern'd ;
Besides, the prince is all for the land-service,
Forgetting Duncan, Nelson, Howe, and Jervis.

V

Brave men were living before Agamemnon
    And since, exceeding valorous and sage,
A good deal like him too, though quite the same none ;
    But then they shone not on the poet's page,
And so have been forgotten :—I condemn none,
    But can't find any in the present age
Fit for my poem (that is, for my new one) ;
So, as I said, I'll take my friend Don Juan.

VI

Most epic poets plunge ' in medias res '
    (Horace makes this the heroic turnpike road),
And then your hero tells, whene'er you please,
    What went before—by way of episode,
While seated after dinner at his ease,
    Beside his mistress in some soft abode,
Palace, or garden, paradise, or cavern,
Which serves the happy couple for a tavern.

VII

That is the usual method, but not mine—
    My way is to begin with the beginning ;
The regularity of my design
    Forbids all wandering as the worst of sinning,
And therefore I shall open with a line
    (Although it cost me half an hour in spinning),
Narrating somewhat of Don Juan's father,
And also of his mother, if you 'd rather.

VIII

In Seville was he born, a pleasant city,
    Famous for oranges and women—he
Who has not seen it will be much to pity,
    So says the proverb—and I quite agree ;
Of all the Spanish towns is none more pretty,
    Cadiz, perhaps—but that you soon may see :—
Don Juan's parents lived beside the river.
A noble stream, and call'd the Guadalquivir.

IX

His father's name was José—*Don*, of course,
    A true Hidalgo, free from every stain
Of Moor or Hebrew blood, he traced his source
    Through the most Gothic gentlemen of Spain ;

A better cavalier n'er mounted horse,
  Or, being mounted, e'er got down again,
Than José, who begot our hero, who
Begot—but that's to come——Well, to renew :

X

His mother was a learned lady, famed
  For every branch of every science known—
In every Christian language ever named,
  With virtues equall'd by her wit alone ;
She made the cleverest people quite ashamed,
  And even the good with inward envy groan,
Finding themselves so very much exceeded
In their own way by all the things that she did.

XI

Her memory was a mine : she knew by heart
  All Calderon and greater part of Lopé,
So that if any actor miss'd his part
  She could have served him for the prompter's copy ;
For her Feinagle's were an useless art,
  And he himself obliged to shut up shop—he
Could never make a memory so fine as
That which adorn'd the brain of Donna Inez.

XII

Her favourite science was the mathematical,
  Her noblest virtue was her magnanimity ;
Her wit (she sometimes tried at wit) was Attic all,
  Her serious sayings darken'd to sublimity ;
In short, in all things she was fairly what I call
  A prodigy—her morning dress was dimity,
Her evening silk, or, in the summer, muslin,
And other stuffs, with which I won't stay puzzling.

XIII

She knew the Latin—that is, 'the Lord's prayer,'
  And Greek—the alphabet—I'm nearly sure ;
She read some French romances here and there,
  Although her mode of speaking was not pure ;
For native Spanish she had no great care,
  At least her conversation was obscure ;
Her thoughts were theorems, her words a problem,
As if she deem'd that mystery would ennoble 'em.

XIV

She liked the English and the Hebrew tongue,
  And said there was analogy between 'em ;
She proved it somehow out of sacred song,
  But I must leave the proofs to those who 've seen 'em,
But this I heard her say, and can't be wrong,
  And all may think which way their judgments lean 'en
' 'T is strange—the Hebrew noun which means " I am."
The English always use to govern d—n.'

Some women use their tongues—she *look'd* a lecture,
  Each eye a sermon, and her brow a homily,
An all-in-all sufficient self-director,
  Like the lamented late Sir Samuel Romilly,
The Law's expounder, and the State's corrector,
  Whose suicide was almost an anomaly—
One sad example more, that ' All is vanity,'—
(The jury brought their verdict in ' Insanity.')

XVI

In short, she was a walking calculation,
  Miss Edgeworth's novels stepping from their covers,
Or Mrs. Trimmer's books on education,
  Or ' Cœleb's Wife ' set out in quest of lovers,
Morality's prim personification,
  In which not Envy's self a flaw discovers ;
To others' share let ' female errors fall,'
For she had not even one—the worst of all.

Oh ! she was perfect past all parallel—
  Of any modern female saint's comparison ;
So far above the cunning power of hell,
  Her guardian angel had given up his garrison ;
Even her minutest motions went as well
  As those of the best time-piece made by Harrison
In virtues nothing earthly can surpass her,
Save thine ' incomparable oil,' Macassar !

XVIII

Perfect she was, but as perfection is
  Insipid in this naughty world of ours,
Where our first parents never learn'd to kiss
  Till they were exiled from their earlier bowers,

Where all was peace, and innocence, and bliss
   (I wonder how they got through the twelve hours),
Don José, like a lineal son of Eve,
Went plucking various fruit without her leave.

XIX

He was a mortal of the careless kind,
   With no great love for learning, or the learn'd,
Who chose to go where'er he had a mind,
   And never dream'd his lady was concern'd ;
The world, as usual, wickedly inclined
   To see a kingdom or a house o'erturn'd,
Whisper'd he had a mistress, some said *two*,
But for domestic quarrels *one* will do.

XX

Now Donna Inez had, with all her merit,
   A great opinion of her own good qualities ;
Neglect, indeed, requires a saint to bear it,
   And such, indeed, she was in her moralities ;
But then she had a devil of a spirit,
   And sometimes mixed up fancies with realities,
And let few opportunities escape
Of getting her liege lord into a scrape.

XXI

This was an easy matter with a man
   Oft in the wrong, and never on his guard ;
And even the wisest, do the best they can,
   Have moments, hours, and days, so unprepared,
That you might ' brain them with their lady's fan ; '
   And sometimes ladies hit exceeding hard,
And fans turn into falchions in fair hands,
And why and wherefore no one understands.

XXII

'T is pity learned virgins ever wed
   With persons of no sort of education,
Or gentlemen, who, though well born and bred,
   Grow tired of scientific conversation ;
I do n't choose to say much upon this head,
   I'm a plain man, and in a single station,
But—Oh ! ye lords of ladies intellectual,
Inform us truly, have they not hen-peck'd you all ?

XXIII

Don José and his lady quarrell'd—*why*,
  Not any of the many could divine,
Though several thousand people chose to try,
  'T was surely no concern of theirs nor mine ;
I loathe that low vice—curiosity ;
  But if there's anything in which I shine,
'T is in arranging all my friends' affairs,
Not having, of my own, domestic cares.

XXIV

And so I interfered, and with the best
  Intentions, but their treatment was not kind ;
I think the foolish people were possess'd,
  For neither of them could I ever find,
Although their porter afterwards confess'd—
  But that's no matter, and the worst 's behind,
For little Juan o'er me threw, downstairs,
A pail of housemaid's water unawares.

XXV

A little curly-headed, good-for-nothing,
  And mischief-making monkey from his birth ;
His parents ne'er agreed except in doting
  Upon the most unquiet imp on earth ;
Instead of quarrelling, had they been but both in
  Their senses, they'd have sent young master forth
To school, or had him soundly whipp'd at home,
To teach him manners for the time to come.

XXVI

Don José and the Donna Inez led
  For some time an unhappy sort of life,
Wishing each other, not divorced, but dead ;
  They lived respectably as man and wife,
Their conduct was exceedingly well-bred,
  And gave no outward signs of inward strife,
Until at length the smother'd fire broke out,
And put the business past all kind of doubt.

XXVII

For Inez call'd some druggists and physicians,
  And tried to prove her loving lord was *mad*,
But as he had some lucid intermissions,
  She next decided he was only *bad* ;

Yet when they ask'd her for her depositions,
    No sort of explanation could be had,
Save that her duty both to man and God,
Required this conduct—which seem'd very odd.

XXVIII

She kept a journal, where his faults were noted,
    And open'd certain trunks of books and letters,
All which might, if occasion served, be quoted ;
    And then she had all Seville for abettors,
Besides her good old grandmother (who doted) ;
    The hearers of her case became repeaters,
Then advocates, inquisitors, and judges,
Some for amusement, others for old grudges.

XXIX

And then this best and meekest woman bore
    With such serenity her husband's woes,
Just as the Spartan ladies did of yore,
    Who saw their spouses killed, and nobly chose
Never to say a word about them more—
    Calmly she heard each calumny that rose,
And saw *his* agonies with such sublimity,
That all the world exclaim'd, ' What magnanimity ! '

XXX

No doubt this patience, when the world is damning us,
    Is philosophic in our former friends ;
'T is also pleasant to be deem'd magnanimous,
    The more so in obtaining our own ends ;
And what the lawyers call a ' *malus animus* '
    Conduct like this by no means comprehends :
Revenge in person 's certainly no virtue,
But then 't is not *my* fault, if *others* hurt you.

XXXI

And if our quarrels should rip up old stories,
    And help them with a lie or two additional,
I'm not to blame, as you well know—no more is
    Any one else—they were become traditional ;
Besides, their resurrection aids our glories
    By contrast, which is what we just were wishing all :
And science profits by this resurrection—
Dead scandals form good subjects for dissection.

XXXII

Their friends had tried at reconciliation,
    Then their relations, who made matters worse,
('T were hard to tell upon a like occasion
    To whom it may be best to have recourse—
I can't say much for friend or yet relation) :
    The lawyers did their utmost for divorce,
But scarce a fee was paid on either side
Before, unluckily, Don José died.

He died ; and most unluckily, because,
    According to all hints I could collect
From counsel learned in those kinds of laws
    (Although their talk 's obscure and circumspect),
His death contrived to spoil a charming cause ;
    A thousand pities also with respect
To public feeling, which on this occasion
Was manifested in a great sensation.

XXXIV

But ah ! he died ; and buried with him lay
    The public feeling and the lawyers' fees :
His house was sold, his servants sent away,
    A Jew took one of his two mistresses,
A priest the other—at least so they say ;
    I ask'd the doctors after his disease—
He died of the slow fever called the tertian,
And left his widow to her own aversion.

Yet José was an honourable man,
    That I must say, who knew him very well ;
Therefore his frailties I 'll no further scan,
    Indeed there were not many more to tell :
And if his passions now and then outran
    Discretion, and were not so peaceable
As Numa's (who was also named Pompilius),
He had been ill brought up, and was born bilious.

XXXVI

Whate'er might be his worthlessness or worth,
    Poor fellow ! he had many things to wound him,
Let 's own—since it can do no good on earth—
    It was a trying moment that which found him

Standing alone beside his desolate hearth,
    Where all his household gods lay shiver'd round him :
No choice was left his feelings or his pride,
Save death or Doctors' Commons—so he died.

XXXVII

Dying intestate, Juan was sole heir
    To a chancery suit, and messuages and lands,
Which, with a long minority and care,
    Promised to turn out well in proper hands :
Inez became sole guardian, which was fair,
    And answer'd but to nature's just demands ;
An only son left with an only mother
Is brought up much more wisely than another.

XXXVIII

Sagest of women, even of widows, she
    Resolved that Juan should be quite a paragon,
And worthy of the noblest pedigree :
    (His sire was of Castile, his dam from Aragon).
Then for accomplishments of chivalry,
    In case our lord the king should go to war again,
He learn'd the arts of riding, fencing, gunnery,
And how to scale a fortress—or a nunnery.

XXXIX

But that which Donna Inez most desired,
    And saw into herself each day before all
The learned tutors whom for him she hired,
    Was, that his breeding should be strictly moral :
Much into all his studies she inquired,
    And so they were submitted first to her, all,
Arts, sciences, no branch was made a mystery
To Juan's eyes, excepting natural history.

XL

The languages, especially the dead,
    The sciences, and most of all the abstruse,
The arts, at least all such as could be said
    To be the most remote from common use,
In all these he was much and deeply read :
    But not a page of anything that 's loose,
Or hints continuation of the species,
Was ever suffer'd, lest he should grow vicious.

XLI

His classic studies made a little puzzle,
  Because of filthy loves of gods and goddesses,
Who in the earlier ages raised a bustle,
  But never put on pantaloons or bodices ;
His reverend tutors had at time a tussle,
  And for their Æneids, Iliads, and Odysseys,
Were forced to make an odd sort of apology,
For Donna Inez dreaded the Mythology.

Ovid's a rake, as half his verses show him,
  Anacreon's morals are a still worse sample,
Catullus scarcely has a decent poem,
  I do n't think Sappho's Ode a good example,
Although Longinus tells us there is no hymn
  Where the sublime soars forth on wings more ample ;
But Virgil's songs are pure, except that horrid one
Beginning with ' Formosum Pastor Corydon.'

XLIII

Lucretius' irreligion is too strong
  For early stomachs, to prove wholesome food ;
I can't help thinking Juvenal was wrong,
  Although no doubt his real intent was good,
For speaking out so plainly in his song,
  So much indeed as to be downright rude ;
And then what proper person can be partial
To all those nauseous epigrams of Martial ?

Juan was taught from out the best edition,
  Expurgated by learned men, who place,
Judiciously, from out the schoolboy's vision,
  The grosser parts ; but fearful to deface
Too much their modest bard by this omission,
  And pitying sore this mutilated case,
They only add them all in an appendix,
Which saves, in fact, the trouble of an index ;

XLV

For there we have them all ' at one fell swoop,'
  Instead of being scatter'd through the pages ;
They stand forth marshall'd in a handsome troop,
  To meet the ingenuous youth of future ages,

Till some less rigid editor shall stoop
    To call them back into their separate cages,
Instead of standing staring all together,
Like garden gods—and not so decent either.

XLVI

The Missal too (it was the family Missal)
    Was ornamented in a sort of way
Which ancient mass-books often are, and this all
    Kinds of grotesques illumined ; and how they
Who saw those figures on the margin kiss all,
    Could turn their optics to the text and pray,
Is more than I know—But Don Juan's mother
Kept this herself, and gave her son another.

XLVII

Sermons he read, and lectures he endured,
    And homilies, and lives of all the saints ;
To Jerome and to Chrysostom inured,
    He did not take such studies for restraints ;
But how faith is acquired, and then insured,
    So well not one of the aforesaid paints
As Saint Augustine in his fine Confessions,
Which make the reader envy his transgressions.

XLVIII

This, too, was a seal'd book to little Juan—
    I can't but say that his mamma was right,
If such an education was the true one.
    She scarcely trusted him from out her sight ;
Her maids were old, and if she took a new one,
    You might be sure she was a perfect fright,
She did this during even her husband's life—
I recommend as much to every wife.

XLIX

Young Juan wax'd in godliness and grace ;
    At six a charming child, and at eleven
With all the promise of as fine a face
    As e'er to man's maturer growth was given.
He studied steadily and grew apace,
    And seem'd, at least, in the right road to heaven,
For half his days were pass'd at church, the other
Between his tutors, confessor, and mother.

L

At six, I said, he was a charming child,
    At twelve he was a fine, but quiet boy ;
Although in infancy a little wild,
    They tamed him down amongst them : to destroy
His natural spirit not in vain they toil'd,
    At least it seem'd so ; and his mother's joy
Was to declare how sage, and still, and steady,
Her young philosopher was grown already.

LI

I had my doubts, perhaps I have them still,
    But what I say is neither here nor there :
I knew his father well, and have some skill
    In character—but it would not be fair
From sire to son to augur good or ill :
    He and his wife were an ill sorted pair—
But scandal's my aversion—I protest
Against all evil speaking, even in jest.

LII

For my part I say nothing—nothing—but
    This I will say—my reasons are my own—
That if I had an only son to put
    To school (as God be praised that I have none),
'T is not with Donna Inez I would shut
    Him up to learn his catechism alone,
No—no—I 'd send him out betimes to college,
For there it was I pick'd up my own knowledge.

LIII

For there one learns—'t is not for me to boast,
    Though I acquired—but I pass over *that*,
As well as all the Greek I since have lost :
    I say that there's the place—but ' *Verbum sat,*'
I think I pick'd up too, as well as most,
    Knowledge of matters—but no matter *what*—
I never married—but, I think, I know
That sons should not be educated so.

LIV

Young Juan now was sixteen years of age,
    Tall, handsome, slender, but well knit : he seem'd
Active, though not so sprightly, as a page ;
    And everybody but his mother deem'd

Him almost man ; but she flew in a rage
  And bit her lips (for else she might have scream'd)
If any said so, for to be precocious
Was in her eyes a thing the most atrocious.

LV

Amongst her numerous acquaintance, all
  Selected for discretion and devotion,
There was the Donna Julia, whom to call
  Pretty were but to give a feeble notion
Of many charms in her as natural
  As sweetness to the flower, or salt to ocean,
Her zone to Venus, or his bow to Cupid,
(But this last simile is trite and stupid).

LVI

The darkness of her Oriental eye
  Accorded with her Moorish origin ;
(Her blood was not all Spanish, by the by ;
  In Spain, you know, this is a sort of sin).
When proud Granada fell, and, forced to fly,
  Boabdil wept, of Donna Julia's kin
Some went to Africa, some stay'd in Spain,
Her great great grandmamma chose to remain.

LVII

She married (I forget the pedigree)
  With an Hidalgo, who transmitted down
His blood less noble than such blood should be ;
  At such alliances his sires would frown,
In that point so precise in each degree
  That they breed *in and in*, as might be shown,
Marrying their cousins—nay, their aunts, and nieces,
Which always spoils the breed, if it increases.

LVIII

This heathenish cross restored the breed again,
  Ruin'd its blood, but much improved its flesh ;
For from a root the ugliest in old Spain
  Sprung up a branch as beautiful as fresh ;
The sons no more were short, the daughters plain :
  But there 's a rumour which I fain would hush,
'T is said that Donna Julia's grandmamma
Produced her Don more heirs at love than law.

89

However this might be, the race went on
   Improving still through every generation,
Until it centred in an only son,
   Who left an only daughter ; my narration
May have suggested that this single one
   Could be but Julia (whom on this occasion
I shall have much to speak about), and she
Was married, charming, chaste, and twenty-three.

Her eye (I'm very fond of handsome eyes)
   Was large and dark, suppressing half its fire
Until she spoke, then through its soft disguise
   Flash'd an expression more of pride than ire,
And love than either ; and there would arise
   A something in them, which was not desire,
But would have been, perhaps, but for the soul
Which struggled through and chasten'd down the whole.

Her glossy hair was cluster'd o'er a brow
   Bright with intelligence, and fair, and smooth ;
Her eyebrow's shape was like the aërial bow,
   Her cheek all purple with the beam of youth,
Mounting, at times, to a transparent glow,
   As if her veins ran lightning ; she, in sooth,
Possess'd an air and grace by no means common :
Her stature tall—I hate a dumpy woman.

Wedded she was some years, and to a man
   Of fifty, and such husbands are in plenty ;
And yet, I think, instead of such a ONE
   'T were better to have TWO of five-and-twenty,
Especially in countries near the sun :
   And now I think on 't, ' mi vien in mente,'
Ladies even of the most uneasy virtue
Prefer a spouse whose age is short of thirty.

'T is a sad thing, I cannot choose but say,
   And all the fault of that indecent sun,
Who cannot leave alone our helpless clay,
   But will keep baking, broiling, burning on,

That howsoever people fast and pray,
    The flesh is frail, and so the soul undone :
What men call gallantry, and gods adultery,
Is much more common where the climate's sultry.

LXIV

Happy the nations of the moral North !
    Where all is virtue, and the winter season
Sends sin, without a rag on, shivering forth
    ('T was snow that brought St. Anthony to reason) ;
Where juries cast up what a wife is worth,
    By laying whate'er sum, in mulct, they please on
The lover, who must pay a handsome price,
Because it is a marketable vice.

LXV

Alfonso was the name of Julia's lord,
    A man well looking for his years, and who
Was neither much beloved nor yet abhorr'd :
    They lived together as most people do,
Suffering each other's foibles by accord,
    And not exactly either *one* or *two* ;
Yet he was jealous, though he did not show it,
For jealousy dislikes the world to know it.

LXVI

Julia was—yet I never could see why—
    With Donna Inez quite a favourite friend ;
Between their tastes there was small sympathy,
    For not a line had Julia ever penn'd :
Some people whisper (but, no doubt, they lie,
    For malice still imputes some private end)
That Inez had, ere Don Alfonso's marriage,
Forgot with him her very prudent carriage ;

LXVII

And that still keeping up the old connexion,
    Which time had lately render'd much more chaste,
She took his lady also in affection,
    And certainly this course was much the best :
She flatter'd Julia with her sage protection,
    And complimented Don Alfonso's taste ;
And if she could not (who can ?) silence scandal,
At least she left it a more slender handle.

I can't tell whether Julia saw the affair
With other people's eyes, or if her own
Discoveries made, but none could be aware
Of this, at least no symptom e'er was shown ;
Perhaps she did not know, or did not care,
Indifferent from the first, or callous grown :
I 'm really puzzled what to think or say,
She kept her counsel in so close a way.

Juan she saw, and, as a pretty child,
Caress'd him often—such a thing might be
Quite innocently done, and harmless styled,
When she had twenty years, and thirteen he ;
But I am not so sure I should have smiled
When he was sixteen, Julia twenty-three ;
These few short years make wondrous alterations,
Particularly amongst sun-burnt nations.

Whate'er the cause might be, they had become
Changed ; for the dame grew distant, the youth shy,
Their looks cast down, their greetings almost dumb,
And much embarrassment in either eye ;
There surely will be little doubt with some
That Donna Julia knew the reason why,
But as for Juan, he had no more notion
Than he who never saw the sea of ocean.

Yet Julia's very coldness still was kind,
And tremulously gentle her small hand
Withdrew itself from his, but left behind
A little pressure, thrilling, and so bland
And slight, so very slight, that to the mind
'T was but a doubt ; but ne'er magician's wand
Wrought change with all Armida's fairy art
Like what this light touch left on Juan's heart.

And if she met him, though she smiled no more,
She look'd a sadness sweeter than her smile,
As if her heart had deeper thoughts in store
She must not own, but cherish'd more the while

For that compression in its burning core ;
  Even innocence itself has many a wile,
And will not dare to trust itself with truth,
And love is taught hypocrisy from youth.

But passion most dissembles, yet betrays
  Even by its darkness ; as the blackest sky
Foretells the heaviest tempest, it displays
  Its workings through the vainly guarded eye,
And in whatever aspect it arrays
  Itself, 't is still the same hypocrisy :
Coldness or anger, even disdain or hate,
Are masks it often wears, and still too late.

Then there were sighs, the deeper for suppression,
  And stolen glances, sweeter for the theft,
And burning blushes, though for no transgression,
  Tremblings when met, and restlessness when left ;
All these are little preludes to possession,
  Of which young passion cannot be bereft,
And merely tend to show how greatly love is
Embarrass'd at first starting with a novice.

Poor Julia's heart was in an awkward state :
  She felt it going, and resolved to make
The noblest efforts for herself and mate,
  For honour's, pride's, religion's, virtue's sake.
Her resolutions were most truly great
  And almost might have made a Tarquin quake :
She pray'd the Virgin Mary for her grace,
As being the best judge of a lady's case.

She vow'd she never would see Juan more,
  And next day paid a visit to his mother,
And look'd extremely at the opening door,
  Which, by the Virgin's grace, let in another ;
Grateful she was, and yet a little sore—
  Again it opens, it can be no other,
'T is surely Juan now—No ! I 'm afraid
That night the Virgin was no further pray'd.

She now determined that a virtuous woman
   Should rather face and overcome temptation,
That flight was base and dastardly, and no man
   Should ever give her heart the least sensation ;
That is to say a thought beyond the common
   Preference, that we must feel upon occasion,
For people who are pleasanter than others,
But then they only seem so many brothers.

And even if by chance—and who can tell ?
   The devil 's so very sly—she should discover
That all within was not so very well,
   And, if still free, that such or such a lover
Might please perhaps, a virtuous wife can quell
   Such thoughts, and be the better when they 're over ;
And if the man should ask, 't is but denial :
I recommend young ladies to make trial.

And then there are such things as love divine,
   Bright and immaculate, unmix'd and pure,
Such as the angels think so very fine,
   And matrons, who would be no less secure,
Platonic, perfect, ' just such love as mine : '
   Thus Julia said—and thought so, to be sure ;
And so I'd have her think, were I the man
On whom her reveries celestial ran.

Such love is innocent, and may exist
   Between young persons without any danger :
A hand may first, and then a lip be kist ;
   For my part, to such doings I 'm a stranger,
But *hear* these freedoms form the utmost list
   Of all o'er which such love may be a ranger :
If people go beyond, 't is quite a crime,
But not my fault—I tell them all in time.

Love, then, but love within its proper limits,
   Was Julia's innocent determination
In young Don Juan's favour, and to him its
   Exertion might be useful on occasion ;

And lighted at too pure a shrine to dim its
     Ethereal lustre, with what sweet persuasion
He might be taught, by love and her together—
I really do n't know what, nor Julia either.

LXXXII

Fraught with this fine intention, and well fenced
     In mail of proof—her purity of soul,
She, for the future of her strength convinced,
     And that her honour was a rock, or mole,
Exceedingly sagely from that hour dispensed
     With any kind of troublesome control ;
But whether Julia to the task was equal
Is that which must be mention'd in the sequel.

LXXXIII

Her plan she deem'd both innocent and feasible,
     And, surely, with a stripling of sixteen
Not scandal's fangs could fix on much that 's seizable,
     Or if they did so, satisfied to mean
Nothing but what was good, her breast was peaceable
     A quiet conscience makes one so serene !
Christians have burnt each other, quite persuaded
That all the Apostles would have done as they did.

LXXXIV

And if in the mean time her husband died,
     But Heaven forbid that such a thought should cross
Her brain, though in a dream ! (and then she sigh'd)
     Never could she survive that common loss ;
But just suppose that moment should betide,
     I only say suppose it—*inter nos*.
(This should be *entre nous*, for Julia thought
In French, but then the rhyme would go for nought.)

LXXXV

I only say, suppose this supposition :
     Juan being then grown up to man's estate
Would fully suit a widow of condition,
     Even seven years hence it would not be too late ;
And in the interim (to pursue this vision)
     The mischief, after all, could not be great,
For he would learn the rudiments of love,
I mean the seraph way of those above.

So much for Julia. Now we 'll turn to Juan.
  Poor little fellow ! he had no idea
Of his own case, and never hit the true one ;
  In feelings quick as Ovid's Miss Medea,
He puzzled over what he found a new one,
  But not as yet imagined it could be a
Thing quite in course, and not at all alarming,
Which, with a little patience, might grow charming.

Silent and pensive, idle, restless, slow,
  His home deserted for the lonely wood,
Tormented with a wound he could not know,
  His, like all deep grief, plunged in solitude :
I'm fond myself of solitude or so,
  But then, I beg it may be understood,
By solitude I mean a Sultan's, not
A hermit's, with a haram for a grot.

' Oh Love ! in such a wilderness as this,
  Where transport and security entwine,
Here is the empire of thy perfect bliss,
  And here thou art a god indeed divine.'
The bard I quote from does not sing amiss,
  With the exception of the second line,
For that same twining ' transport and security '
Are twisted to a phrase of some obscurity.

The poet meant, no doubt, and thus appeals
  To the good sense and senses of mankind,
The very thing which everybody feels,
  As all have found on trial, or may find,
That no one likes to be disturb'd at meals
  Or love.—I won't say more about ' entwined '
Or ' transport,' as we knew all that before,
But beg ' Security ' will bolt the door.

Young Juan wander'd by the glassy brooks,
  Thinking unutterable things ; he threw
Himself at length within the leafy nooks
  Where the wild branch of the cork forest grew ;

There poets find materials for their books,
  And every now and then we read them through,
So that their plan and prosody are eligible,
Unless, like Wordsworth, they prove unintelligible.

XCI

He, Juan (and not Wordsworth), so pursued
  His self-communion with his own high soul,
Until his mighty heart, in its great mood,
  Had mitigated part, though not the whole
Of its disease ; he did the best he could
  With things not very subject to control,
And turn'd, without perceiving his condition,
Like Coleridge, into a metaphysician.

XCII

He thought about himself, and the whole earth,
  Of man the wonderful, and of the stars,
And how the deuce they ever could have birth ;
  And then he thought of earthquakes, and of wars,
How many miles the moon might have in girth,
  Of air-balloons, and of the many bars
To perfect knowledge of the boundless skies ;—
And then he thought of Donna Julia's eyes.

XCIII

In thoughts like these true wisdom may discern
  Longings sublime, and aspirations high,
Which some are born with, but the most part learn
  To plague themselves withal, they know not why :
'Twas strange that one so young should thus concern
  His brain about the action of the sky ;
If *you* think 't was philosophy that this did,
I can't help thinking puberty assisted.

XCIV

He pored upon the leaves, and on the flowers,
  And heard a voice in all the winds ; and then
He thought of wood-nymphs and immortal bowers,
  And how the goddesses came down to men :
He miss'd the pathway, he forgot the hours,
  And when he look'd upon his watch again,
He found how much old Time had been a winner—
He also found that he had lost his dinner.

Sometimes he turn'd to gaze upon his book,
    Boscan, or Garcilasso ;—by the wind
Even as the page is rustled while we look,
    So by the poesy of his own mind
Over the mystic leaf his soul was shook,
    As if 't were one whereon magicians bind
Their spells, and give them to the passing gale
According to some good old woman's tale.

Thus would he while his lonely hours away
    Dissatisfied, nor knowing what he wanted ;
Nor glowing reverie, nor poet's lay,
    Could yield his spirit that for which it panted,
A bosom whereon he his head might lay,
    And hear the heart beat with the love it granted,
With——several other things, which I forget,
Or which, at least, I need not mention yet.

Those lonely walks, and lengthening reveries,
    Could not escape the gentle Julia's eyes ;
She saw that Juan was not at his ease ;
    But that which chiefly may, and must surprise,
Is, that the Donna Inez did not tease
    Her only son with question or surmise ;
Whether it was she did not see, or would not,
Or, like all very clever people, could not.

This may seem strange, but yet 't is very common ;
    For instance—gentlemen, whose ladies take
Leave to o'erstep the written rights of woman,
    And break the——Which commandment is 't they brea
(I have forgot the number, and think no man
    Should rashly quote, for fear of a mistake.)
I say, when these same gentlemen are jealous,
They make some blunder, which their ladies tell us.

A real husband always is suspicious,
    But still no less suspects in the wrong place,
Jealous of some one who had no such wishes,
    Or pandering blindly to his own disgrace,

By harbouring some dear friend extremely vicious;
  The last indeed 's infallibly the case :
And when the spouse and friend are gone off wholly,
He wonders at their vice, and not his folly.

C

Thus parents also are at times short-sighted ;
  Though watchful as the lynx, they ne'er discover,
The while the wicked world beholds delighted,
  Young Hopeful's mistress, or Miss Fanny's lover,
Till some confounded escapade has blighted
  The plan of twenty years, and all is over ;
And then the mother cries, the father swears,
And wonders why the devil he got heirs.

CI

But Inez was so anxious, and so clear
  Of sight, that I must think, on this occasion,
She had some other motive much more near
  For leaving Juan to this new temptation,
But what that motive was, I shan't say here ;
  Perhaps to finish Juan's education,
Perhaps to open Don Alfonso's eyes,
In case he thought his wife too great a prize.

CII

It was upon a day, a summer's day ;—
  Summer's indeed a very dangerous season,
And so is spring about the end of May ;
  The sun, no doubt, is the prevailing reason ;
But whatsoe'er the cause is, one may say,
  And stand convicted of more truth than treason,
That there are months which nature grows more merry in,—
March has its hares, and May must have its heroine.

CIII

'T was on a summer's day—the sixth of June :—
  I like to be particular in dates,
Not only of the age, and year, but moon ;
  They are a sort of post-house, where the Fates
Change horses, making history change its tune,
  Then spur away o'er empires and o'er states,
Leaving at last not much besides chronology,
Excepting the post-obits of theology.

'T was on the sixth of June, about the hour
    Of half-past six—perhaps still nearer seven—
When Julia sate within as pretty a bower
    As e'er held houri in that heathenish heaven
Described by Mahomet, and Anacreon Moore,
    To whom the lyre and laurels have been given,
With all the trophies of triumphant song—
He won them well, and may he wear them long !

She sate, but not alone ; I know not well
    How this same interview had taken place,
And even if I knew, I should not tell—
    People should hold their tongues in any case ;
No matter how or why the thing befell,
    But there were she and Juan, face to face—
When two such faces are so, 't would be wise,
But very difficult to shut their eyes.

How beautiful she look'd ! her conscious heart
    Glow'd in her cheek, and yet she felt no wrong.
Oh Love ! how perfect is thy mystic art,
    Strengthening the weak, and trampling on the strong !
How self-deceitful is the sagest part
    Of mortals whom thy lure hath led along !—
The precipice she stood on was immense,
So was her creed in her own innocence.

She thought of her own strength, and Juan's youth,
    And of the folly of all prudish fears,
Victorious virtue, and domestic truth,
    And then of Don Alfonso's fifty years :
I wish these last had not occurr'd, in sooth,
    Because that number rarely much endears,
And through all climes, the snowy and the sunny,
Sounds ill in love, what'er it may in money.

When people say, ' I 've told you *fifty* times,'
    They mean to scold, and very often do ;
When poets say, ' I 've written *fifty* rhymes,'
    They make you dread that they'll recite them too ;

In gangs of *fifty*, thieves commit their crimes ;
   At *fifty* love for love is rare, 't is true,
But then, no doubt, it equally as true is,
A good deal may be bought for *fifty* Louis.

CIX

Julia had honour, virtue, truth, and love
   For Don Alfonso ; and she inly swore,
By all the vows below to powers above,
   She never would disgrace the ring she wore,
Nor leave a wish which wisdom might reprove ;
   And while she ponder'd this, besides much more,
One hand on Juan's carelessly was thrown,
Quite by mistake—she thought it was her own ;

CX

Unconsciously she lean'd upon the other,
   Which play'd within the tangles of her hair ;
And to contend with thoughts she could not smother
   She seem'd, by the distraction of her air.
'T was surely very wrong in Juan's mother
   To leave together this imprudent pair,
She who for many years had watch'd her son so—
I 'm very certain *mine* would not have done so.

CXI

The hand which still held Juan's, by degrees
   Gently, but palpably confirm'd its grasp,
As if it said, ' Detain me, if you please ; '
   Yet there 's no doubt she only meant to clasp
His fingers with a pure Platonic squeeze ;
   She would have shrunk as from a toad, or asp,
Had she imagined such a thing could rouse
A feeling dangerous to a prudent spouse.

CXII

I cannot know what Juan thought of this,
   But what he did, is much what you would do ;
His young lip thank'd it with a grateful kiss,
   And then, abash'd at its own joy, withdrew
In deep despair, lest he had done amiss,—
   Love is so very timid when 't is new :
She blush'd, and frown'd not, but she strove to speak,
And held her tongue, her voice was grown so weak.

The sun set, and up rose the yellow moon :
    The devil's in the moon for mischief ; they
Who call'd her CHASTE, methinks, began too soon
    Their nomenclature ; there is not a day,
The longest, not the twenty-first of June,
    Sees half the business in a wicked way,
On which three single hours of moonshine smile—
And then she looks so modest all the while.

CXIV

There is a dangerous silence in that hour,
    A stillness, which leaves room for the full soul
To open all itself, without the power
    Of calling wholly back its self-control ;
The silver light which, hallowing tree and tower,
    Sheds beauty and deep softness o'er the whole,
Breathes also to the heart, and o'er it throws
A loving languor, which is not repose.

CXV

And Julia sate with Juan, half embraced
    And half retiring from the glowing arm,
Which trembled like the bosom where 't was placed ;
    Yet still she must have thought there was no harm,
Or else 't were easy to withdraw her waist ;
    But then the situation had its charm,
And then——God knows what next—I can't go on ;
I'm almost sorry that I e'er begun.

CXVI

Oh Plato ! Plato ! you have paved the way,
    With your confounded fantasies, to more
Immoral conduct by the fancied sway
    Your system feigns o'er the controlless core
Of human hearts, than all the long array
    Of poets and romancers :—You 're a bore,
A charlatan, a coxcomb—and have been,
At best, no better than a go-between.

CXVII

And Julia's voice was lost, except in sighs,
    Until too late for useful conversation ;
The tears were gushing from her gentle eyes,
    I wish, indeed, they had not had occasion ;

But who, alas ! can love, and then be wise ?
　　Not that remorse did not oppose temptation ;
A little still she strove, and much repented,
And whispering ' I will ne'er consent '—consented.

CXVIII

'T is said that Xerxes offer'd a reward
　　To those who could invent him a new pleasure :
Methinks the requisition's rather hard,
　　And must have cost his majesty a treasure :
For my part, I 'm a moderate-minded bard,
　　Fond of a little love (which I call leisure) ;
I care not for new pleasures, as the old
Are quite enough for me, so they but hold.

CXIX

Oh Pleasure ! you 're indeed a pleasant thing,
　　Although one must be damn'd for you, no doubt :
I make a resolution every spring
　　Of reformation, ere the year run out,
But somehow, this my vestal vow takes wing,
　　Yet still, I trust, it may be kept throughout :
I 'm very sorry, very much ashamed,
And mean, next winter, to be quite reclaim'd.

CXX

Here my chaste Muse a liberty must take—
　　Start not ! still chaster reader—she 'll be nice hence-
Forward, and there is no great cause to quake ;
　　This liberty is a poetic licence,
Which some irregularity may make
　　In the design, and as I have a high sense
Of Aristotle and the Rules, 't is fit
To beg his pardon when I err a bit.

CXXI

This licence is to hope the reader will
　　Suppose from June the sixth (the fatal day
Without whose epoch my poetic skill
　　For want of facts would all be thrown away),
But keeping Julia and Don Juan still
　　In sight, that several months have pass'd ; we'll say
'T was in November, but I'm not so sure
About the day—the era's more obscure.

CXXII

We 'll talk of that anon,—'T is sweet to hear
    At midnight on the blue and moonlit deep
The song and oar of Adria's gondolier,
    By distance mellow'd, o'er the waters sweep ;
'T is sweet to see the evening star appear ;
    'T is sweet to listen as the night-winds creep
From leaf to leaf ; 't is sweet to view on high
The rainbow, based on ocean, span the sky.

CXXIII

'T is sweet to hear the watch-dog's honest bark
    Bay deep-mouth'd welcome as we draw near home ;
'T is sweet to know there is an eye will mark
    Our coming, and look brighter when we come ;
'T is sweet to be awaken'd by the lark,
    Or lull'd by falling waters ; sweet the hum
Of bees, the voice of girls, the song of birds,
The lisp of children, and their earliest words.

CXXIV

Sweet is the vintage, when the showering grapes
    In Bacchanal profusion reel to earth,
Purple and gushing ; sweet are our escapes
    From civic revelry to rural mirth ;
Sweet to the miser are his glittering heaps,
    Sweet to the father is his first-born's birth,
Sweet is revenge—especially to women,
Pillage to soldiers, prize-money to seamen.

CXXV

Sweet is a legacy, and passing sweet
    The unexpected death of some old lady
Or gentleman of seventy years complete,
    Who 've made ' us youth ' wait too—too long already
For an estate, or cash, or country seat,
    Still breaking, but with stamina so steady
That all the Israelites are fit to mob its
Next owner for their double-damn'd post-obits.

CXXVI

'T is sweet to win, no matter how, one's laurels,
    By blood or ink ; 't is sweet to put an end
To strife ; 't is sometimes sweet to have our quarrels,
    Particularly with a tiresome friend :

Sweet is old wine in bottles, ale in barrels ;
  Dear is the helpless creature we defend
Against the world ; and dear the schoolboy spot
We ne'er forget, though there we are forgot.

CXXVII

But sweeter still than this, than these, than all,
  Is first and passionate love—it stands alone,
Like Adam's recollection of his fall ;
  The tree of knowledge has been pluck'd—all 's known—
And life needs nothing further to recall
  Worthy of this ambrosial sin, so shown,
No doubt in fable, as the unforgiven
Fire which Prometheus filch'd for us from heaven.

CXXVIII

Man 's a strange animal, and makes strange use
  Of his own nature, and the various arts,
And likes particularly to produce
  Some new experiment to show his parts ;
This is the age of oddities let loose,
  Where different talents find their different marts ;
You 'd best begin with truth, and when you 've lost your
Labour, there 's a sure market for imposture.

CXXIX

What opposite discoveries we have seen !
  (Signs of true genius, and of empty pockets.)
One makes new noses, one a guillotine,
  One breaks your bones, one sets them in their sockets ;
But vaccination certainly has been
  A kind antithesis to Congreve's rockets,
With which the Doctor paid off an old pox,
By borrowing a new one from an ox.

CXXX

Bread has been made (indifferent) from potatoes ;
  And galvanism has set some corpses grinning,
But has not answer'd like the apparatus
  Of the Humane Society's beginning,
By which men are unsuffocated gratis :
  What wondrous new machines have late been spinning !
I said the small pox has gone out of late ;
Perhaps it may be follow'd by the great.

CXXXI

'T is said the great came from America ;
　　Perhaps it may set out on its return,—
The population there so spreads, they say
　　'T is grown high time to thin it in its turn,
With war, or plague, or famine, any way,
　　So that civilisation they may learn ;
And which in ravage the more loathsome evil is—
Their real lues, or our pseudo-syphilis ?

CXXXII

This is the patent age of new inventions
　　For killing bodies, and for saving souls,
All propagated with the best intentions ;
　　Sir Humphry Davy's lantern, by which coals
Are safely mined for in the mode he mentions,
　　Timbuctoo travels, voyages to the Poles,
Are ways to benefit mankind, as true,
Perhaps, as shooting them at Waterloo.

CXXXIII

Man 's a phenomenon, one knows not what,
　　And wonderful beyond all wondrous measure ;
'T is pity though, in this sublime world, that
　　Pleasure 's a sin, and sometimes sin 's a pleasure ;
Few mortals know what end they would be at,
　　But whether glory, power, or love, or treasure,
The path is through perplexing ways, and when
The goal is gain'd, we die, you know—and then——

CXXXIV

What then ?—I do not know, no more do you—
　　And so good night.—Return we to our story :
'T was in November, when fine days are few,
　　And the far mountains wax a little hoary,
And clap a white cape on their mantles blue ;
　　And the sea dashes round the promontory,
And the loud breaker boils against the rock,
And sober suns must set at five o'clock.

CXXXV

'T was, as the watchmen say, a cloudy night ;
　　No moon, no stars, the wind was low or loud
By gusts, and many a sparkling hearth was bright
　　With the piled wood, round which the family crowd ;

There 's something cheerful in that sort of light,
    Even as a summer sky 's without a cloud :
I 'm fond of fire, and crickets, and all that,
A lobster salad, and champagne, and chat.

CXXXVI

'T was midnight—Donna Julia was in bed,
    Sleeping, most probably,—when at her door
Arose a clatter might awake the dead,
    If they had never been awoke before,
And that they have been so we all have read,
    And are to be so, at the least once more ;—
The door was fasten'd, but with voice and fist
First knocks were heard, then ' Madam—Madam—hist !

CXXXVII

' For God's sake, Madam—Madam—here 's my master,
    With more than half the city at his back—
Was ever heard of such a curst disaster !
    'T is not my fault—I kept good watch—Alack !
Do pray undo the bolt a little faster—
    They're on the stair just now, and in a crack
Will all be here ; perhaps he yet may fly—
Surely the window's not so *very* high ! '

CXXXVIII

By this time Don Alfonso was arrived,
    With torches, friends, and servants in great number ;
The major part of them had long been wived,
    And therefore paused not to disturb the slumber
Of any wicked woman, who contrived
    By stealth her husband's temples to encumber :
Examples of this kind are so contagious,
Were *one* not punish'd, *all* would be outrageous.

CXXXIX

I can't tell how, or why, or what suspicion
    Could enter into Don Alfonso's head ;
But for a cavalier of his condition
    It surely was exceedingly ill-bred,
Without a word of previous admonition,
    To hold a levee round his lady's bed,
And summon lackeys, arm'd with fire and sword,
To prove himself the thing he most abhorr'd.

Poor Donna Julia ! starting as from sleep
   (Mind—that I do not say—she had not slept),
Began at once to scream, and yawn, and weep ;
   Her maid, Antonia, who was an adept,
Contrived to fling the bed-clothes in a heap,
   As if she had just now from out them crept :
I can't tell why she should take all this trouble
To prove her mistress had been sleeping double.

But Julia mistress, and Antonia maid,
   Appear'd like two poor harmless women, who
Of goblins, but still more of men afraid,
   Had thought one man might be deterr'd by two,
And therefore side by side were gently laid,
   Until the hours of absence should run through,
And truant husband should return, and say,
'My dear, I was the first who came away.'

Now Julia found at length a voice, and cried,
   'In heaven's name, Don Alfonso, what d'ye mean ?
Has madness seized you ? would that I had died
   Ere such a monster's victim I had been !
What may this midnight violence betide,
   A sudden fit of drunkenness or spleen ?
Dare you suspect me, whom the thought would kill ?
Search, then, the room !'—Alfonso said, 'I will.'

He search'd, *they* search'd, and rummaged everywhere,
   Closet and clothes-press, chest and window-seat,
And found much linen, lace, and several pair
   Of stockings, slippers, brushes, combs, complete,
With other articles of ladies fair,
   To keep them beautiful, or leave them neat :
Arras they prick'd and curtains with their swords,
And wounded several shutters, and some boards.

Under the bed they search'd, and there they found—
   No matter what—it was not that they sought ;
They open'd windows, gazing if the ground
   Had signs or footmarks, but the earth said nought

And then they stared each other's faces round :
　'T is odd, not one of all these seekers thought,
And seems to me almost a sort of blunder,
Of looking *in* the bed as well as under.

CXLV

During this inquisition Julia's tongue
　Was not asleep—' Yes, search and search,' she cried,
' Insult on insult heap, and wrong on wrong !
　It was for this that I became a bride !
For this in silence I have suffer'd long
　A husband like Alfonso at my side ;
But now I 'll bear no more, nor here remain,
If there be law or lawyers in all Spain.

CXLVI

' Yes, Don Alfonso ! husband now no more,
　If ever you indeed deserved the name,
Is 't worthy of your years ?—you have three-score—
　Fifty, or sixty, it is all the same—
Is 't wise or fitting, causeless to explore
　For facts against a virtuous woman's fame ?
Ungrateful, perjured, barbarous Don Alfonso,
How dare you think your lady would go on so ?

CXLVII

' Is it for this I have disdain'd to hold
　The common privileges of my sex ?
That I have chosen a confessor so old
　And deaf, that any other it would vex,
And never once he has had cause to scold,
　But found my very innocence perplex
So much, he always doubted I was married—
How sorry you will be when I 've miscarried !

CXLVIII

' Was it for this that no Cortejo e'er
　I yet have chosen from out the youth of Seville ?
Is it for this I scarce went anywhere,
　Except to bull-fights, mass, play, rout, and revel ?
Is it for this, whate'er my suitors were,
　I favour'd none—nay, was almost uncivil ?
Is it for this that General Count O'Reilly,
Who took Algiers, declares I used him vilely ?

CXLIX

' Did not the Italian Musico Cazzani
   Sing at my heart six months at least in vain ?
Did not his countryman, Count Corniani,
   Call me the only virtuous wife in Spain ?
Were there not also Russians, English, many ?
   The Count Strongstroganoff I put in pain,
And Lord Mount Coffeehouse, the Irish peer,
Who kill'd himself for love (with wine) last year.

CL

' Have I not had two bishops at my feet ?
   The Duke of Ichar, and Don Fernan Nunez ?
And is it thus a faithful wife you treat ?
   I wonder in what quarter now the moon is :
I praise your vast forbearance not to beat
   Me also, since the time so opportune is—
Oh, valiant man ! with sword drawn and cock'd trigger,
Now, tell me, don't you cut a pretty figure ?

CLI

' Was it for this you took your sudden journey,
   Under pretence of business indispensable,
With that sublime of rascals your attorney,
   Whom I see standing there, and looking sensible
Of having play'd the fool ? though both I spurn, he
   Deserves the worst, his conduct 's less defensible,
Because, no doubt, 't was for his dirty fee,
And not from any love to you nor me.

CLII

' If he comes here to take a deposition,
   By all means let the gentleman proceed ;
You've made the apartment in a fit condition :—
   There's pen and ink for you, sir, when you need—
Let everything be noted with precision,
   I would not you for nothing should be fee'd—
But as my maid 's undrest, pray turn your spies out.'
' Oh ! ' sobb'd Antonia, ' I could tear their eyes out.'

CLIII

' There is the closet, there the toilet, there
   The antechamber—search them under, over ;
There is the sofa, there the great arm-chair,
   The chimney—which would really hold a lover.

I wish to sleep, and beg you will take care
  And make no further noise, till you discover
The secret cavern of this lurking treasure—
And when 't is found, let me, too, have that pleasure.

CLIV

' And now, Hidalgo ! now that you have thrown
  Doubt upon me, confusion over all,
Pray have the courtesy to make it known
  Who is the man you search for ? how d' ye call
Him ? what's his lineage ? let him but be shown—
  I hope he's young and handsome—is he tall ?
Tell me—and be assured, that since you stain
Mine honour thus, it shall not be in vain.

CLV

' At least, perhaps, he has not sixty years,
  At that age he would be too old for slaughter,
Or for so young a husband's jealous fears—
  (Antonia ! let me have a glass of water.)
I am ashamed of having shed these tears,
  They are unworthy of my father's daughter ;
My mother dream'd not in my natal hour,
That I should fall into a monster's power.

CLVI

' Perhaps 't is of Antonia you are jealous,
  You saw that she was sleeping by my side,
When you broke in upon us with your fellows ;
  Look where you please—we 've nothing, sir, to hide ;
Only another time, I trust, you 'll tell us,
  Or for the sake of decency abide
A moment at the door, that we may be
Drest to receive so much good company.

CLVII

' And now, sir, I have done, and say no more ;
  The little I have said may serve to show
The guileless heart in silence may grieve o'er
  The wrongs to whose exposure it is slow :—
I leave you to your conscience as before,
  'T will one day ask you, *why* you used me so ?
God grant you feel not then the bitterest grief !
Antonia ! where 's my pocket-handkerchief ? '

She ceased, and turn'd upon her pillow ; pale
   She lay, her dark eyes flashing through their tears,
Like skies that rain and lighten ; as a veil,
   Waved and o'ershading her wan cheek, appears
Her streaming hair ; the black curls strive, but fail,
   To hide the glossy shoulder, which uprears
Its snow through all ;—her soft lips lie apart,
And louder than her breathing beats her heart.

CLIX

The Senhor Don Alfonso stood confused ;
   Antonia bustled round the ransack'd room,
And, turning up her nose, with looks abused
   Her master, and his myrmidons, of whom
Not one, except the attorney, was amused ;
   He, like Achates, faithful to the tomb,
So there were quarrels, cared not for the cause,
Knowing they must be settled by the laws.

CLX

With prying snub-nose, and small eyes, he stood,
   Following Antonia's motions here and there,
With much suspicion in his attitude ;
   For reputations he had little care ;
So that a suit or action were made good,
   Small pity had he for the young and fair,
And ne'er believed in negatives, till these
Were proved by competent false witnesses.

CLXI

But Don Alfonso stood with downcast looks,
   And, truth to say, he made a foolish figure ;
When, after searching in five hundred nooks,
   And treating a young wife with so much rigour,
He gain'd no point, except some self-rebukes,
   Added to those his lady with such vigour
Had pour'd upon him for the last half hour,
Quick, thick, and heavy—as a thunder shower.

CLXII

At first he tried to hammer an excuse,
   To which the sole reply was tears and sobs,
And indications of hysterics, whose
   Prologue is always certain throes, and throbs,

Gasps, and whatever else the owners choose :
  Alfonso saw his wife, and thought of Job's ;
He saw too, in perspective, her relations,
And then he tried to muster all his patience.

CLXIII

He stood in act to speak, or rather stammer,
  But sage Antonia cut him short before
The anvil of his speech received the hammer,
  With ' Pray, sir, leave the room, and say no more,
Or madam dies.'—Alfonso mutter'd, ' D—n her,'
  But nothing else, the time of words was o'er ;
He cast a rueful look or two, and did,
He knew not wherefore, that which he was bid.

CLXIV

With him retired his ' *posse comitatus*,'
  The attorney last, who linger'd near the door
Reluctantly, still tarrying there as late as
  Antonia let him—not a little sore
At this most strange and unexplain'd ' *hiatus* '
  In Don Alfonso's facts, which just now wore
An awkward look ; as he revolved the case,
The door was fastened in his legal face.

CLXV

No sooner was it bolted, than—Oh shame !
  Oh sin ! Oh sorrow ! and Oh womankind !
How can you do such things and keep your fame,
  Unless this world, and t' other too, be blind ?
Nothing so dear as an unfilch'd good name !
  But to proceed—for there is more behind
With much heartfelt reluctance be it said,
Young Juan slipp'd, half-smother'd, from the bed.

CLXVI

He had been hid—I don't pretend to say
  How, nor can I indeed describe the where—
Young, slender, and pack'd easily, he lay,
  No doubt, in little compass, round or square ;
But pity him I neither must nor may
  His suffocation by that pretty pair ;
'T were better, sure, to die so, than be shut
With maudlin Clarence in his Malmsey butt.

And, secondly, I pity not, because
    He had no business to commit a sin,
Forbid by heavenly, fined by human laws,
    At least 't was rather early to begin ;
But at sixteen the conscience rarely gnaws
    So much as when we call our old debts in
At sixty years, and draw the accompts of evil,
And find a deuced balance with the devil.

CLXVIII

Of his position I can give no notion :
    'T is written in the Hebrew Chronicle,
How the physicians, leaving pill and potion,
    Prescribed, by way of blister, a young belle,
When old King David's blood grew dull in motion,
    And that the medicine answer'd very well ;
Perhaps 't was in a different way applied,
For David lived, but Juan nearly died.

CLXIX

What 's to be done ?   Alfonso will be back
    The moment he has sent his fools away.
Antonia's skill was put upon the rack,
    But no device could be brought into play—
And how to parry the renew'd attack ?
    Besides, it wanted but few hours of day :
Antonia puzzled ; Julia did not speak,
But press'd her bloodless lip to Juan's cheek.

CLXX

He turn'd his lip to hers, and with his hand
    Call'd back the tangles of her wandering hair ;
Even then their love they could not all command,
    And half forgot their danger and despair :
Antonia's patience now was at a stand—
    ' Come, come, 't is no time now for fooling there,'
She whisper'd, in great wrath—' I must deposit
This pretty gentleman within the closet :

CLXXI

' Pray, keep your nonsense for some luckier night—
    Who can have put my master in this mood ?
What will become on 't—I 'm in such a fright,
    The devil 's in the urchin, and no good—

Is this a time for giggling ? this a plight ?
  Why, do n't you know that it may end in blood ?
You 'll lose your life, and I shall lose my place,
My mistress all, for that half-girlish face.

CLXXII

' Had it but been for a stout cavalier
  Of twenty-five or thirty—(come, make haste)
But for a child, what piece of work is here !
  I really, madam, wonder at your taste—
(Come, sir, get in)—my master must be near :
  There, for the present, at the least, he 's fast,
And if we can but till the morning keep
Our counsel—Juan, mind, you must not sleep.'

CLXXIII

Now, Don Alfonso entering, but alone,
  Closed the oration of the trusty maid :
She loiter'd, and he told her to be gone,
  An order somewhat sullenly obey'd ;
However, present remedy was none,
  And no great good seem'd answer'd if she staid ;
Regarding both with slow and sidelong view,
She snuff'd the candle, curtsied, and withdrew.

CLXXIV

Alfonso paused a minute—then begun
  Some strange excuses for his late proceeding :
He would not justify what he had done,
  To say the best, it was extreme ill-breeding ;
But there were ample reasons for it, none
  Of which he specified in this his pleading :
His speech was a fine sample, on the whole,
Of rhetoric, which the learn'd call ' *rigmarole*.'

CLXXV

Julia said nought ; though all the while there rose
  A ready answer, which at once enables
A matron, who her husband's foible knows,
  By a few timely words to turn the tables,
Which, if it does not silence, still must pose,—
  Even if it should comprise a pack of fables ;
'T is to retort with firmness, and when he
Suspects with *one*, do you reproach with *three*.

CLXXVI

Julia, in fact, had tolerable grounds,—
  Alfonso's loves with Inez were well known ;
But whether 't was that one's own guilt confounds—
  But that can't be, as has been often shown,
A lady with apologies abounds ;—
  It might be that her silence sprang alone
From delicacy to Don Juan's ear,
To whom she knew his mother's fame was dear.

CLXXVII

There might be one more motive, which makes two,
  Alfonso ne'er to Juan had alluded,—
Mentioned his jealousy, but never who
  Had been the happy lover, he concluded,
Conceal'd amongst his premises ; 't is true,
  His mind the more o'er this its mystery brooded
To speak of Inez now were, one may say,
Like throwing Juan in Alfonso's way.

CLXXVIII

A hint, in tender cases, is enough ;
  Silence is best : besides there is a *tact*—
(That modern phrase appears to me sad stuff,
  But it will serve to keep my verse compact)—
Which keeps, when push'd by questions rather rough
  A lady always distant from the fact :
The charming creatures lie with such a grace,
There 's nothing so becoming to the face.

CLXXIX

They blush, and we believe them ; at least I
  Have always done so ; 't is of no great use,
In any case, attempting a reply,
  For then their eloquence grows quite profuse ;
And when at length they're out of breath, they sigh,
  And cast their languid eyes down, and let loose
A tear or two, and then we make it up ;
And then—and then—and then—sit down and sup.

CLXXX

Alfonso closed his speech, and begged her pardon,
  Which Julia half withheld, and then half granted,
And laid conditions he thought very hard, on,
  Denying several little things he wanted :

He stood like Adam lingering near his garden,
    With useless penitence perplex'd and haunted,
Beseeching she no further would refuse,
When, lo ! he stumbled o'er a pair of shoes.

CLXXXI

A pair of shoes !—what then ? not much, if they
    Are such as fit with ladies' feet, but these
(No one can tell how much I grieve to say)
    Were masculine ; to see them, and to seize,
Was but a moment's act.—Ah ! well-a-day !
    My teeth begin to chatter, my veins freeze—
Alfonso first examined well their fashion,
And then flew out into another passion.

CLXXXII

He left the room for his relinquish'd sword,
    And Julia instant to the closet flew.
' Fly, Juan, fly ! for heaven's sake—not a word—
    The door is open—you may yet slip through
The passage you so often have explored—
    Here is the garden-key—Fly—fly—Adieu !
Haste—haste ! I hear Alfonso's hurrying feet—
Day has not broke—there 's no one in the street.'

CLXXXIII

None can say that this was not good advice,
    The only mischief was, it came too late ;
Of all experience 't is the usual price,
    A sort of income-tax laid on by fate :
Juan had reach'd the room-door in a trice,
    And might have done so by the garden-gate,
But met Alfonso in his dressing-gown,
Who threaten'd death—so Juan knock'd him down.

CLXXXIV

Dire was the scuffle, and out went the light ;
    Antonia cried out ' Rape ! ' and Julia ' Fire ! '
But not a servant stirr'd to aid the fight.
    Alfonso, pommell'd to his heart's desire,
Swore lustily he 'd be revenged this night ;
    And Juan, too, blasphemed an octave higher ;
His blood was up : though young, he was a Tartar,
And not at all disposed to prove a martyr.

Alfonso's sword had dropp'd ere he could draw it,
    And they continued battling hand to hand,
For Juan very luckily ne'er saw it ;
    His temper not being under great command,
If at that moment he had chanced to claw it,
    Alfonso's days had not been in the land
Much longer.—Think of husbands', lovers' lives !
And how ye may be doubly widows—wives !

Alfonso grappled to detain the foe,
    And Juan throttled him to get away,
And blood ('t was from the nose) began to flow ;
    At last, as they more faintly wrestling lay,
Juan contrived to give an awkward blow,
    And then his only garment quite gave way ;
He fled, like Joseph, leaving it ; but there,
I doubt, all likeness ends between the pair.

Lights came at length, and men, and maids, who found
    An awkward spectacle their eyes before ;
Antonia in hysterics, Julia swoon'd,
    Alfonso, leaning, breathless, by the door ;
Some half-torn drapery scatter'd on the ground,
    Some blood, and several footsteps, but no more :
Juan the gate gain'd, turn'd the key about,
And liking not the inside, lock'd the out.

Here ends this canto.—Need I sing, or say,
    How Juan, naked, favour'd by the night,
Who favours what she should not, found his way,
    And reach'd his home in an unseemly plight ?
The pleasant scandal which arose next day,
    The nine days' wonder which was brought to light,
And how Alfonso sued for a divorce,
Were in the English newspapers, of course.

If you would like to see the whole proceedings,
    The depositions and the cause at full,
The names of all the witnesses, the pleadings
    Of counsel to nonsuit, or to annul,

There's more than one edition, and the readings
    Are various, but they none of them are dull;
The best is that in short-hand ta'en by Gurney,
Who to Madrid on purpose made a journey.

CXC

But Donna Inez, to divert the train
    Of one of the most circulating scandals
That had for centuries been known in Spain,
    At least, since the retirement of the Vandals,
First vow'd (and never had she vow'd in vain)
    To Virgin Mary several pounds of candles;
And then, by the advice of some old ladies,
She sent her son to be shipp'd off from Cadiz.

CXCI

She had resolved that he should travel through
    All European climes, by land or sea,
To mend his former morals, and get new,
    Especially in France and Italy
(At least this is the thing most people do).
    Julia was sent into a convent: she
Grieved, but, perhaps, her feelings may be better
Shown in the following copy of her Letter:—

CXCII

'They tell me 't is decided you depart:
    'T is wise—'t is well, but not the less a pain;
I have no further claim on your young heart,
    Mine is the victim, and would be again:
To love too much has been the only art
    I used:—I write in haste, and if a stain
Be on this sheet, 't is not what it appears;
My eyeballs burn and throb, but have no tears.

CXCIII

'I loved, I love you, for this love have lost
    State, station, heaven, mankind's, my own esteem,
And yet cannot regret what it hath cost,
    So dear is still the memory of that dream;
Yet, if I name my guilt, 't is not to boast,
    None can deem harshlier of me than I deem:
I trace this scrawl because I cannot rest—
I 've nothing to reproach or to request.

119

' Man's love is of Man's life a thing apart,
   'T is woman's whole existence ; man may range
The court, camp, church, the vessel, and the mart ;
   Sword, gown, gain, glory, offer in exchange
Pride, fame, ambition, to fill up his heart,
   And few there are whom these cannot estrange ;
Men have all these resources, we but one,
To love again, and be again undone.

CXCV

' You will proceed in pleasure, and in pride,
   Beloved and loving many ; all is o'er
For me on earth, except some years to hide
   My shame and sorrow deep in my heart's core :
These I could bear, but cannot cast aside
   The passion which still rages as before,—
And so farewell—forgive me, love me—No,
That word is idle now—but let it go.

CXCVI

' My breast has been all weakness, is so yet ;
   But still I think I can collect my mind ;
My blood still rushes where my spirit's set,
   As roll the waves before the settled wind ;
My heart is feminine, nor can forget—
   To all, except one image, madly blind ;
So shakes the needle, and so stands the pole,
As vibrates my fond heart to my fix'd soul.

CXCVII

' I have no more to say, but linger still,
   And dare not set my seal upon this sheet,
And yet I may as well the task fulfil,
   My misery can scarce be more complete :
I had not lived till now, could sorrow kill ;
   Death shuns the wretch who fain the blow would meet
And I must even survive this last adieu,
And bear with life, to love and pray for you ! '

CXCVIII

This note was written upon gilt-edged paper
   With a neat little crow-quill, slight and new ;
Her small white hand could hardly reach the taper,
   It trembled as magnetic needles do,

And yet she did not let one tear escape her;
  The seal a sun-flower; '*Elle vous suit partout,*'
The motto, cut upon a white cornelian;
The wax was superfine, its hue vermilion.

CXCIX

This was Don Juan's earliest scrape; but whether
  I shall proceed with his adventures is
Dependent on the public altogether;
  We 'll see, however, what they say to this,
Their favour in an author's cap 's a feather,
  And no great mischief's done by their caprice;
And if their approbation we experience,
Perhaps they 'll have some more about a year hence.

CC

My poem 's epic, and is meant to be
  Divided in twelve books; each book containing,
With love, and war, a heavy gale at sea,
  A list of ships, and captains, and kings reigning,
New characters; the episodes are three:
  A panoramic view of hell 's in training,
After the style of Virgil and of Homer,
So that my name of Epic 's no misnomer.

CCI

All these things will be specified in time,
  With strict regard to Aristotle's rules,
The *Vade Mecum* of the true sublime,
  Which makes so many poets, and some fools:
Prose poets like blank-verse, I'm fond of rhyme,
  Good workmen never quarrel with their tools;
I 've got new mythological machinery,
And very handsome supernatural scenery.

CCII

There 's only one slight difference between
  Me and my epic brethren gone before,
And here the advantage is my own, I ween
  (Not that I have not several merits more,
But this will more peculiarly be seen);
  They so embellish, that 't is quite a bore
Their labyrinth of fables to thread through,
Whereas this story's actually true.

CCIII

If any person doubt it, I appeal
    To history, tradition, and to facts
To newspapers, whose truth all know and feel,
    To plays in five, and operas in three acts ;
All these confirm my statement a good deal,
    But that which more completely faith exacts
Is, that myself, and several now in Seville,
Saw Juan's last elopement with the devil.

CCIV

If ever I should condescend to prose,
    I 'll write poetical commandments, which
Shall supersede beyond all doubt all those
    That went before ; in these I shall enrich
My text with many things that no one knows,
    And carry precept to the highest pitch :
I 'll call the work ' Longinus o'er a Bottle,
Or, Every Poet his *own* Aristotle.'

CCV

Thou shalt believe in Milton, Dryden, Pope ;
    Thou shalt not set up Wordsworth, Coleridge, Southey ;
Because the first is crazed beyond all hope,
    The second drunk, the third so quaint and mouthy :
With Crabbe it may be difficult to cope,
    And Campbell's Hippocrene is somewhat drouthy :
Thou shalt not steal from Samuel Rogers, nor
Commit—flirtation with the muse of Moore.

CCVI

Thou shalt not covet Mr. Sotheby's Muse,
    His Pegasus, nor anything that 's his ;
Thou shalt not bear false witness like ' the Blues '—
    (There 's one, at least, is very fond of this) ;
Thou shalt not write, in short, but what I choose ;
    This is true criticism, and you may kiss—
Exactly as you please, or not,—the rod ;
But if you do n't, I 'll lay it on, by G—d !

CCVII

If any person should presume to assert
    This story is not moral, first, I pray,
That they will not cry out before they're hurt,
    Then that they 'll read it o'er again, and say

(But, doubtless, nobody will be so pert),
  That this is not a moral tale, though gay ;
Besides, in Canto Twelfth, I mean to show
The very place where wicked people go.

CCVIII

If, after all, there should be some so blind
  To their own good this warning to despise,
Led by some tortuosity of mind,
  Not to believe my verse and their own eyes,
And cry that they ' the moral cannot find,'
  I tell him, if a clergyman, he lies ;
Should captains the remark, or critics, make,
They also lie too—under a mistake.

CCIX

The public approbation I expect,
  And beg they 'll take my word about the moral,
Which I with their amusement will connect
  (So children cutting teeth receive a coral) ;
Meantime they 'll doubtless please to recollect
  My epical pretensions to the laurel :
For fear some prudish readers should grow skittish,
I 've bribed my grandmother's review—the British.

CCX

I sent it in a letter to the Editor,
  Who thank'd me duly by return of post—
I 'm for a handsome article his creditor ;
  Yet, if my gentle Muse he please to roast,
And break a promise after having made it her,
  Denying the receipt of what it cost,
And smear his page with gall instead of honey,
All I can say is—that he had the money.

CCXI

I think that with this holy new alliance
  I may ensure the public, and defy
All other magazines of art or science,
  Daily, or monthly, or three monthly ; I
Have not essay'd to multiply their clients,
  Because they tell me 't were in vain to try,
And that the Edinburgh Review and Quarterly
Treat a dissenting author very martyrly.

' *Non ego hoc ferrem calida juventa*
    Consule Planco,' Horace said, and so
Say I ; by which quotation there is meant a
    Hint that some six or seven good years ago
(Long ere I dreamt of dating from the Brenta)
    I was most ready to return a blow,
And would not brook at all this sort of thing
In my hot youth—when George the Third was King.

CCXIII

But now at thirty years my hair is gray—
    (I wonder what it will be like at forty ?
I thought of a peruke the other day—)
    My heart is not much greener ; and, in short, I
Have squander'd my whole summer while 't was May,
    And feel no more the spirit to retort : I
Have spent my life, both interest and principal,
And deem not, what I deem'd, my soul invincible.

CCXIV

No more—no more—Oh ! never more on me
    The freshness of the heart can fall like dew,
Which out of all the lovely things we see
    Extracts emotions beautiful and new ;
Hived in our bosoms like the bag o' the bee.
    Think'st thou the honey with those objects grew ?
Alas ! 't was not in them, but in thy power
To double even the sweetness of a flower.

CCXV

No more—no more—Oh ! never more, my heart,
    Canst thou be my sole world, my universe !
Once all in all, but now a thing apart,
    Thou canst not be my blessing or my curse :
The illusion 's gone for ever, and thou art
    Insensible, I trust, but none the worse,
And in thy stead I 've got a deal of judgment,
Though heaven knows how it ever found a lodgment.

CCXVI

My days of love are over ; me no more
    The charms of maid, wife, and still less of widow,
Can make the fool of which they made before,—
    In short, I must not lead the life I did do ;

The credulous hope of mutual minds is o'er,
  The copious use of claret is forbid too,
So for a good old-gentlemanly vice,
I think I must take up with avarice.

CCXVII

Ambition was my idol, which was broken
  Before the shrines of Sorrow, and of Pleasure ;
And the two last have left me many a token
  O'er which reflection may be made at leisure ;
Now, like Friar Bacon's brazen head, I 've spoken,
  ' Time is, Time was, Time's past : '—a chymic treasure
Is glittering youth, which I have spent betimes—
My heart in passion, and my head on rhymes.

CCXVIII

What is the end of fame ? 't is but to fill
  A certain portion of uncertain paper :
Some liken it to climbing up a hill,
  Whose summit, like all hills, is lost in vapour ;
For this men write, speak, preach, and heroes kill,
  And bards burn what they call their ' midnight taper.'
To have, when the original is dust,
A name, a wretched picture, and worse bust.

CCXIX

What are the hopes of man ? Old Egypt's King
  Cheops erected the first pyramid
And largest, thinking it was just the thing
  To keep his memory whole, and mummy hid :
But somebody or other rummaging,
  Burglariously broke his coffin's lid :
Let not a monument give you or me hopes,
Since not a pinch of dust remains of Cheops.

CCXX

But I, being fond of true philosophy,
  Say very often to myself, ' Alas !
All things that have been born were born to die,
  And flesh (which Death mows down to hay) is grass ;
You 've passed your youth not so unpleasantly,
  And if you had it o'er again—'t would pass—
So thank your stars that matters are no worse,
And read your Bible, sir, and mind your purse.'

CCXXI

But for the present, gentle reader ! and
 Still gentler purchaser ! the bard—that's I—
Must, with permission, shake you by the hand,
 And so your humble servant, and good-bye !
We meet again, if we should understand
 Each other ; and if not, I shall not try
Your patience further than by this short sample—
'T were well if others follow'd my example.

CCXXII

' Go little book, from this my solitude.
 I cast thee on the waters—go thy ways !
And if, as I believe, thy vein be good,
 The world will find thee after many days.'
When Southey 's read, and Wordsworth understood,
 I can't help putting in my claim to praise—
The four first rhymes are Southey's, every line :
For God's sake, reader ! take them not for mine !

CANTO III

XCI

MILTON's the prince of poets—so we say ;
 A little heavy, but no less divine :
An independent being in his day—
 Learn'd, pious, temperate in love and wine ;
But his life falling into Johnson's way,
 We 're told this great high priest of all the Nine
Was whipt at college—a harsh sire—odd spouse,
For the first Mrs. Milton left his house.

XCII

All these are, *certes*, entertaining facts.
 Like Shakespeare's stealing deer, Lord Bacon's bribes ;
Like Titus' youth, and Cæsar's earliest acts ;
 Like Burns (whom Doctor Currie well describes) ;
Like Cromwell's pranks ;—but although truth exacts
 These amiable descriptions from the scribes,
As most essential to their hero's story,
They do not much contribute to his glory.

XCIII

All are not moralists, like Southey, when
   He prated to the world of ' Pantisocrasy ; '
Or Wordsworth unexcised, unhired, who then
   Season'd his pedlar poems with democracy ;
Or Coleridge, long before his flighty pen
   Let to the Morning Post its aristocracy ;
When he and Southey, following the same path,
Espoused two partners (milliners of Bath).

XCIV

Such names at present cut a convict figure,
   The very Botany Bay in moral geography ;
Their loyal treason, renegado rigour,
   Are good manure for their more bare biography ;
Wordsworth's last quarto, by the way, is bigger
   Than any since the birthday of typography ;
A drowsy frowzy poem, call'd the ' Excursion,'
Writ in a manner which is my aversion.

XCV

He there builds up a formidable dyke
   Between his own and others' intellect :
But Wordsworth's poem, and his followers, like
   Joanna Southcote's Shiloh, and her sect,
Are things which in this century do n't strike
   The public mind,—so few are the elect ;
And the new births of both their stale virginities
Have proved but dropsies, taken for divinities.

*

CANTO IV

CIV

I PASS each day where Dante's bones are laid :
   A little cupola, more neat than solemn,
Protects his dust, but reverence here is paid
   To the bard's tomb, and not the warrior's column :
The time must come, when both alike decay'd,
   The chieftain's trophy, and the poet's volume,
Will sink where lie the songs and wars of earth,
Before Pelides' death, or Homer's birth.

CV

With human blood that column was cemented,
    With human filth that column is defiled,
As if the peasant's coarse contempt were vented
    To show his loathing of the spot he soil'd :
Thus is the trophy used, and thus lamented
    Should ever be those blood-hounds, from whose wile
Instinct of gore and glory earth has known
Those sufferings Dante saw in hell alone.

CVI

Yet there will still be bards : though fame is smoke,
    Its fumes are frankincense to human thought ;
And the unquiet feelings, which first woke
    Song in the world, will seek what then they sought :
As on the beach the waves at last are broke,
    Thus to their extreme verge the passions brought
Dash into poetry, which is but passion,
Or at least was so ere it grew a fashion.

CVII

If in the course of such a life as was
    At once adventurous and contemplative,
Men who partake all passions as they pass,
    Acquire the deep and bitter power to give
Their images again as in a glass,
    And in such colours that they seem to live ;
You may do right forbidding them to show 'em,
But spoil (I think) a very pretty poem.

*

CANTO IX

I

OH, Wellington ! (or ' Villainton '—for Fame
    Sounds the heroic syllables both ways ;
France could not even conquer your great name
    But punn'd it down to this facetious phrase—
Beating or beaten she will laugh the same,)
    You have obtain'd great pensions and much praise :
Glory like yours should any dare gainsay,
Humanity would rise, and thunder ' Nay ! '

II

I do n't think that you used Kinnaird quite well
    In Marinet's affair—in fact 't was shabby,
And like some other things won't do to tell
    Upon your tomb in Westminster's old abbey.
Upon the rest 't is not worth while to dwell,
    Such tales being for the tea-hours of some tabby;
But though your years as *man* tend fast to *zero*,
In fact your grace is still but a *young hero*.

III

Though Britain owes (and pays you too) so much,
    Yet Europe doubtless owes you greatly more:
You have repair'd Legitimacy's crutch,
    A prop not quite so certain as before:
The Spanish, and the French, as well as Dutch,
    Have seen, and felt, how strongly you *restore*;
And Waterloo has made the world your debtor
(I wish your bards would sing it rather better).

IV

You are ' the best of cut-throats:'—do not start;
    The phrase is Shakespeare's, and not misapplied:—
War's a brain-spattering, windpipe slitting art,
    Unless her cause by right be sanctified.
If you have acted *once* a generous part,
    The world, not the world's masters, will decide,
And I shall be delighted to learn who,
Save you and yours, have gain'd by Waterloo?

V

I am no flatterer—you 've supp'd full of flattery:
    They say you like it too—'t is no great wonder.
He whose whole life has been assault and battery,
    At last may get a little tired of thunder;
And swallowing eulogy much more than satire, he
    May like being praised for every lucky blunder,
Call'd ' Saviour of the Nations '—not yet saved,
And ' Europe's Liberator '—still enslaved.

VI

I 've done.   Now go and dine from off the plate
    Presented by the Prince of the Brazils,
And send the sentinel before your gate
    A slice or two from your luxurious meals:

129

He fought, but has not fed so well of late.
    Some hunger, too, they say the people feels :—
There is no doubt that you deserve your ration,
But pray give back a little to the nation.

VII

I do n't mean to reflect—a man so great as
    You, my lord duke ! is far above reflection :
The high Roman fashion, too, of Cincinnatus,
    With modern history has but small connexion ;
Though as an Irishman you love potatoes,
    You need not take them under your direction ;
And half a million for your Sabine farm
Is rather dear !—I 'm sure I mean no harm.

VIII

Great men have always scorn'd great recompenses :
    Epaminondas saved his Thebes, and died,
Not leaving even his funeral expenses :
    George Washington had thanks, and nought beside,
Except the all-cloudless glory (which few men's is)
    To free his country : Pitt too had his pride,
And as a high-soul'd minister of state is
Renown'd for ruining Great Britain gratis.

IX

Never had mortal man such opportunity,
    Except Napoleon, or abused it more :
You might have freed fallen Europe from the unity
    Of tyrants, and been blest from shore to shore :
And *now*—what *is* your fame ? Shall the Muse tune it y
    Now—that the rabble's first vain shouts are o'er ?
Go ! hear it in your famish'd country's cries !
Behold the world ! and curse your victories !

*

CANTO XI

LV

In twice five years the ' greatest living poet,
    Like to the champion in the fisty ring,
Is call'd on to support his claim, or show it,
    Although 't is an imaginary thing.

130

Even I—albeit I 'm sure I did not know it,
    Nor sought of foolscap subjects to be king,—
Was reckon'd, a considerable time,
The grand Napoleon of the realms of rhyme.

LVI

But Juan was my Moscow, and Faliero
    My Leipsic, and my Mont Saint Jean seems Cain :
' La Belle Alliance ' of dunces down at zero,
    Now that the Lion 's fall'n, may rise again :
But I will fall at least as fell my hero ;
    Nor reign at all, or as a *monarch* reign ;
Or to some lonely isle of gaolers go,
With turncoat Southey for my turnkey Lowe.

LVII

Sir Walter reign'd before me ; Moore and Campbell
    Before and after : but now grown more holy,
The Muses upon Sion's hill must ramble
    With poets almost clergymen, or wholly :
And Pegasus has a psalmodic amble
    Beneath the very Reverend Rowley Powley,
Who shoes the glorious animal with stilts,
A modern Ancient Pistol—by the hilts !

LVIII

Still he excels that artificial hard
    Labourer in the same vineyard, though the vine
Yields him but vinegar for his reward,—
    That neutralised dull Dorus of the Nine ;
That swarthy Sporus, neither man nor bard ;
    That ox of verse, who *ploughs* for every line :—
Cambyses' roaring Romans beat at least
The howling Hebrews of Cybele's priest.—

LIX

Then there 's my gentle Euphues ; who, they say,
    Sets up for being a sort of *moral me* ;
He 'll find it rather difficult some day
    To turn out both, or either, it may be.
Some persons think that Coleridge hath the sway ;
    And Wordsworth has supporters, two or three ;
And that deep-mouth'd Bœotian ' Savage Landor '
Has taken for a swan rogue Southey's gander.

LX

John Keats, who was kill'd off by one critique,
  Just as he really promised something great,
If not intelligible, without Greek
  Contrived to talk about the Gods of late,
Much as they might have been supposed to speak,
  Poor fellow! His was an untoward fate;
'T is strange the mind, that fiery particle,
Should let itself be snuff'd out by an article.

The list grows long of live and dead pretenders
  To that which none will gain—or none will know
The conqueror at least; who, ere Time renders
  His last award, will have the long grass grow
Above his burnt-out brain, and sapless cinders.
  If I might augur, I should rate but low
Their chances;—they 're too numerous, like the thirty
Mock tyrants, when Rome's annals wax'd but dirty.

LXII

This is the literary *lower* empire,
  Where the prætorian bands take up the matter;—
A 'dreadful trade,' like his who 'gathers samphire,'
  The insolent soldiery to soothe and flatter,
With the same feelings as you'd coax a vampire.
  Now, were I once at home, and in good satire,
I 'd try conclusions with those Janizaries,
And show them *what* an intellectual war is.

I think I know a trick or two, would turn
  Their flanks;—but it is hardly worth my while
With such small gear to give myself concern:
  Indeed I 've not the necessary bile;
My natural temper 's really aught but stern,
  And even my Muse's worst reproof 's a smile;
And then she drops a brief and modern curtsy,
And glides away, assured she never hurts ye.

*

CANTO XV

XCVII

The night—(I sing by night—sometimes an owl,
   And now and then a nightingale)—is dim,
And the loud shriek of sage Minerva's fowl
   Rattles around me her discordant hymn :
Old portraits from old walls upon me scowl—
   I wish to heaven they would not look so grim ;
The dying embers dwindle in the grate—
I think too that I have sat up too late :

XCVIII

And therefore, though 't is by no means my way
   To rhyme at noon—when I have other things
To think of, if I ever think—I say
   I feel some chilly midnight shudderings,
And prudently postpone, until mid-day,
   Treating a topic which, alas ! but brings
Shadows ;—but you must be in my condition
Before you learn to call this superstition.

XCIX

Between two worlds life hovers like a star,
   'Twixt night and morn, upon the horizon's verge
How little do we know that which we are !
   How less what we may be ! The eternal surge
Of time and tide rolls on, and bears afar
   Our bubbles ; as the old burst, new emerge,
Lash'd from the foam of ages ; while the graves
Of empires heave but like some passing waves.

To WALTER SCOTT   July 6, 1812

I have just been honoured with your letter.—I feel sorry
that you should have thought it worth while to notice the
'evil works of my nonage,' (*English Bards and Scotch
Reviewers*—R.F.) as the thing is suppressed *voluntarily*
and your explanation is too kind not to give me pain. The
Satire was written when I was very young and very angry,
and fully bent on displaying my wrath and my wit, and
now I am haunted by the ghosts of my wholesale assertions.

To THOMAS MOORE   April 9, 1814

No more rhyme for—or rather, *from*—me. I have taken
my leave of that stage, and henceforth will mountebank it
no longer. I have had my day, and there's an end. The
utmost I expect, or even wish, is to have it said in the
Biographia Britannica, that I might perhaps have been a
poet, had I gone on and amended. My great comfort is,
that the temporary celebrity I have wrung from the world
has been in the very teeth of all opinions and prejudices.
I have flattered no ruling powers ; I have never concealed a
single thought that tempted me. They can't say I have
truckled to the times, nor to popular topics (as Johnson, or
somebody, said of Cleveland), and whatever I have gained
has been at the expenditure of as much *personal* favour as
possible ; for I do believe never was a bard more unpopular, *quoad homo*, than myself. And now I have done ;
—*ludite nunc alios*. Everybody may be damned, as they
seem fond of it, and resolve to stickle lustily for endless
brimstone.

Oh—by the by, I had nearly forgot. There is a long
poem, an *Anti-Byron*, coming out, to prove that I have
formed a conspiracy to overthrow, by *rhyme*, all religion
and government, and have already made great progress !
It is not very scurrilous, but serious and ethereal. I never
felt myself important, till I saw and heard of my being
such a little Voltaire as to induce such a production.
Murray would not publish it, for which he was a fool, and
so I told him ; but someone else will, doubtless. 'Something too much of this.'

To Thomas Moore   August 3, 1814

Oh ! I have had the most amusing letter from Hogg, the
Ettrick minstrel and shepherd. He wants me to recommend him to Murray ; and, speaking of his present book-
seller, whose ' bills ' are never ' lifted,' he adds, *totidem
verbis*, ' God damn him and them both.' I laughed, and
so would you too, at the way in which this execration is
introduced. The said Hogg is a strange being, but of
great, though uncouth, powers. I think very highly of
him as a poet ; but he, and half of these Scotch and Lake
troubadours, are spoilt by living in little circles and petty
societies. London and the world is the only place to take
the conceit out of a man—in the milling phrase.

To Leigh Hunt   October 30, 1815

I take leave to differ with you on Wordsworth, as freely
as I once agreed with you ; at that time I gave him credit
for a promise, which is unfulfilled. I still think his capacity
warrants all you say of *it* only, but that his performances
since *Lyrical Ballads* are miserably inadequate to the ability
which lurks within him : there is undoubtedly much
natural talent spilt over the *Excursion ;* but it is rain upon
rocks—where it stands and stagnates, or rain upon sands—
where it falls without fertilising. Who can understand
him ? Let those who do make him intelligible. Jacob
Behman, Swedenborg, and Joanna Southcote, are mere
types of this arch-apostle of mystery and mysticism. But I
have done,—no, I have not done, for I have two petty,
and perhaps unworthy objections in small matters to make
to him, which, with his pretensions to accurate observation,
and fury against Pope's false translation of ' the Moonlight
scene in Homer,' I wonder he should have fallen into ;—
these be they :—He says of Greece in the body of his book—
that it is a land of

> *Rivers, fertile plains*, and *sounding* shores,
> Under a cope of *variegated* sky.

The rivers are dry half the year, the plains are barren, and
the shores *still* and *tideless* as the Mediterranean can make
them ; the sky is anything but variegated, being for
months and months but ' darkly, deeply, beautifully

blue.'—The next is in his notes, where he talks of our
' Monuments crowded together in the busy, etc.,' of a large
town,' as compared with the ' still seclusion of a Turkish
cemetery in some *remote* place.' This is pure stuff; for *one*
monument in our churchyards there are *ten* in the Turkish,
and so crowded, that you cannot walk between them;
that is, divided merely by a path or road; and as to
' *remote* places,' men never take the trouble in a barbarous
country, to carry their dead very far; they must have
lived near to where they were buried . . .

These things I was struck with, as coming peculiarly
in my own way; and in both of these he is wrong; yet
I should have noticed neither, but for his attack on Pope
for a like blunder, and a peevish affectation about him of
despising a popularity which he will never obtain. I write
in great haste, and, I doubt, *not* much to the purpose; but
you have it hot and hot, just as it comes, and so let it go.
By-the-way, both he and you go too far against Pope's
' So when the moon,' etc.; it is no translation, I know;
but it is not such false description as asserted. I have read
it on the spot; there is a burst, and a lightness, and a glow
about the night in the Troad, which makes the ' planets
vivid,' and the ' pole glowing.' The moon is—at least the
sky is, clearness itself; and I know no more appropriate
expression for the expansion of such a heaven—o'er the
scene—the plain—the sky—Ida—the Hellespont—Simois
—Scamander—and the Isles—than that of a ' flood of
glory.'

To THOMAS MOORE   January 28, 1817

I rejoice to hear of your forthcoming in February—
though I tremble for the ' magnificence ' which you
attribute to the new *Childe Harold*. I am glad you like it;
it is a fine indistinct piece of poetical desolation, and my
favourite. I was half mad during the time of its composi-
tion, between metaphysics, mountains, lakes, love unextin-
guishable, thoughts unutterable, and the nightmare of my
own delinquencies. I should, many a good day, have
blown my brains out, but for the recollection that it would
have given pleasure to my mother-in-law; and, even *then*,
if I could have been certain to haunt her—but I won't
dwell upon these trifling family matters.

To JOHN MURRAY   September 15, 1817

With regard to poetry in general, I am convinced, the more I think of it, that he (Thomas Moore—R.F.) and *all* of us—Scott, Southey, Wordsworth, Moore, Campbell, I, —are all in the wrong, one as much as another ; that we are upon a wrong revolutionary poetical system, or systems, not worth a damn in itself, and from which none but Rogers and Crabbe are free ; and that the present and next generations will finally be of this opinion. I am the more confirmed in this by having lately gone over some of our classics, particularly *Pope*, whom I tried in this way,— I took Moore's poems and my own and some others, and went over them side by side with Pope's, and I was really astonished (I ought not to have been so) and mortified at the ineffable distance in point of sense, harmony, effect, and even *Imagination*, passion, and *Invention*, between the little Queen Anne's man, and us of the Lower Empire. Depend upon it, it is all Horace then, and Claudian now, among us ; and if I had to begin again, I would model myself accordingly. Crabbe's the man, but he has got a coarse and impracticable subject, and Rogers, the Grandfather of living poetry, is retired upon half-pay (I don't mean as a Banker).

To THOMAS MOORE   September 19, 1818

I have finished the first canto (a long one, of about 180 octaves) of a poem in the style and manner of *Beppo*, encouraged by the good success of the same. It is called *Don Juan*, and is meant to be quietly facetious upon every thing. But I doubt whether it is not—at least, as far as it has just gone—too free for these very modest days. However, I shall try the experiment, anonymously ; and if it don't take, it will be discontinued. It is dedicated to Southey in good, simple, savage verse, upon the Laureate's politics, and the way he got them. But the bore of copying it out is intolerable . . .

To JOHN MURRAY   November 24, 1818

Lord Lauderdale set off from hence twelve days ago, accompanied by a cargo of poesy (The first canto of *Don Juan*, and other poems—R.F.) directed to Mr. Hobhouse— all spick and span, and in MS. You will see what it is like.

I have given it to Master Southey, and he shall have mor
before I have done with him. I understand the scoundre
said, on his return from Switzerland two years ago, tha
' Shelley and I were in a league of Incest, etc., etc.' He is
burning liar ! for the women to whom he alludes are no
sisters—one being Godwin's daughter, by Mary Woll
stonecraft, and the other daughter of the *present* (second
Mrs. Gn, by a *former* husband ; and in the next place, i
they had even been so, there was no *promiscuous intercours*
whatever.

You may make what I say here as public as you please—
more particularly to Southey, whom I look upon, and wil
say it as publicly, to be a dirty, lying rascal ; and wil
prove it in ink—or in his blood, if I did not believe him
to be too much of a poet to risk it. If he had forty review
at his back—as he has the *Quarterly*—I would have at him
in his scribbling capacity, now that he has begun with me
but I will do nothing underhand. Tell him what I say
from *me*, and everyone else you please.

You will see what I have said if the parcel arrives safe. I
understand *Coleridge* went about repeating Southey's lie
with pleasure. I can believe it, for I had done him what is
called a favour. I can understand Coleridge's abusing me,
but how or why *Southey*—whom I had never obliged in any
sort of way, or done him the remotest service—should go
about fibbing and calumniating is more than I readily
comprehend.

Does he think to put me down with his *canting*—not
being able to do so with his poetry ? We will try the
question. I have read his review of Hunt, where he has
attacked Shelley in an oblique and shabby manner. Does
he know what that review has done ? I will tell you. It
has *sold* an edition of the *Revolt of Islam*, which, otherwise,
nobody would have thought of reading, and few who read
can understand—I for one.

TO JOHN MURRAY   January 25, 1819

If the poem (Cantos I and II of *Don Juan*—R.F.) has
poetry, it would stand ; if not, fall : the rest is ' leather
and prunella,' and has never yet affected any human
production ' pro or con.' Dullness is the only annihilator
in such cases. As to the Cant of the day, I despise it, as I

have ever done all its other finical fashions, which become you as paint became the Antient Britons. If you admit this prudery, you must omit half Ariosto, La Fontaine, Shakespeare, Beaumont, Fletcher, Massinger, Ford, all the Charles Second writers; in short, *something* of most who have written before Pope and are worth reading, and much of Pope himself. *Read him*—most of you *don't*—but *do*— and I will forgive you; though the inevitable consequence would be that you would burn all I have ever written, and all your other wretched Claudians of the day (except Scott and Crabbe) into the bargain. I wrong Claudian, who *was* a *poet*, by naming him with such fellows; but he was the *ultimus Romanorum*, the tail of the Comet, and these persons are the tail of an old Gown cut into a waistcoat for Jackey; but being both *tails*, I have compared one with the other, though very unlike, like all Similies. I write in a passion and a Sirocco, and I was up till six this morning at the Carnival; but I *protest*, as I did in my former letter.

TO JOHN MURRAY   April 6, 1819

So you and Mr. Foscolo, etc., want me to undertake what you call a 'great work'? an Epic poem, I suppose, or some such pyramid. I'll try no such thing; I hate tasks. And then 'seven or eight years!' God send us all well this day three months, let alone years. If one's years can't be better employed than in sweating poesy, a man had better be a ditcher. And works, too!—is *Childe Harold* nothing? You have so many '*divine*' poems, is it nothing to have written a *Human* one? without any of your worn-out machinery. Why, man, I could have spun the thoughts of the four cantos of that poem into twenty, had I wanted to book-make, and its passion into as many modern tragedies. Since you want *length*, you shall have enough of *Juan*, for I'll make 50 cantos. . . .

As to the Estimation of the English which you talk of, let them calculate what it is worth, before they insult me with their insolent condescension.

I have not written for their pleasure. If they are pleased, it is that they choose to be so; I have never flattered their opinions, nor their pride; nor will I. Neither will I make 'Ladies books' *al dilettar le femine e la plebe*. I have written from the fullness of my mind, from passion, from impulse, from many motives, but not for their 'sweet voices.'

I know the precise worth of popular applause, for few Scribblers have had more of it ; and if I chose to swerve into their paths, I could retain it, or resume it, or increase it. But I neither love ye, nor fear ye ; and though I buy with ye and sell with ye, and talk with ye, I will neither eat with ye, drink with ye, nor pray with ye. They made me without my search, a species of popular Idol ; they, without reason or judgement, beyond the caprice of their good pleasure, threw down the Image from its pedestal ; it was not broken with the fall, and they would, it seems, again replace it—but they shall not.

To John Murray   August 12, 1819

You are right, Gifford is right, Crabbe is right, Hobhouse is right—you are all right, and I am all wrong ; but do pray let me have that pleasure. Cut me up root and branch ; quarter me in the *Quarterly ;* send round my *disjecti membra pœtæ,* like those of the Levite's Concubine ; make me, if you will, a spectacle to men and angels ; but don't ask me to alter (*Don Juan*—R.F.), for I can't :—I am obstinate and lazy—and there's the truth.

But, nevertheless, I will answer your friend C(ohen), who objects to the quick succession of fun and gravity, as if in that case the gravity did not (in intention, at least) heighten the fun. His metaphor is, that ' we are never scorched and drenched at the same time.' Blessings on his experience ! Ask him these questions about ' scorching and drenching.' Did he never play at Cricket, or walk a mile in hot weather ? Did he never spill a dish of tea over himself in handing the cup to his charmer, to the great shame of his nankeen breeches ? Did he never swim in the sea at Noonday with the sun in his eyes and on his head, which all the foam of Ocean could not cool ? Did he never draw his foot out of a tub of too hot water, damning his eyes and his valet's ? Was he ever in a Turkish bath, that marble paradise of sherbet and Sodomy ? Was he ever in a cauldron of boiling oil, like St. John ? or in the sulphureous waves of hell ? (where he ought to be for his ' scorching and drenching at the same time '). Did he ever tumble into a river or lake, fishing, and sit in his wet clothes in the boat, or on the bank, afterwards 'scorched and drenched,' like a true sportsman ? 'Oh, for breath to utter !'—but make him my compliments ; he is a clever fellow for all that—a very clever fellow.

You ask me for the plan of Donny Johnny : I *have* no plan—I *had* no plan ; but I have or had materials ; though if, like Tony Lumpkin, I am 'to be snubbed so when I am in spirits,' the poem will be naught, and the poet turn serious again. If it don't take, I will leave it off where it is, with all due respect to the public ; but if continued, it must be in my own way. You might as well make Hamlet (or Diggory) 'act mad' in a straight waistcoat as trammel my buffoonery, if I am to be a buffoon : their gestures and my thoughts would only be pitiably absurd and ludicrously constrained. Why, Man, the Soul of such writing is its licence ; at least the *liberty* of that *licence*, if one likes—*not* that one should abuse it: it is like trial by Jury and Peerage and the Habeas Corpus —a very fine thing but chiefly in the reversion ; because no one wishes to be tried for the mere pleasure of proving his possession of the privilege.

To Richard Belgrave Hoppner   October 29, 1819

Perhaps I did not make myself understood. He (Murray—R.F.) told me the sale (of Cantos I and II of *Don Juan*—R.F.) had not been great—1200 out of 1500 quarto I believe (which is nothing after selling 13000 of *The Corsair* in one day) but that the 'best judges, etc.,' had said it was very fine, and clever, and particularly good English, and poetry, and all those consolatory things which are not, however, worth a single copy to a book-seller ;—and as to the author—of course I am in a damned passion at the bad taste of the times, and swear there is nothing like posterity, who of course must know more of the matter than their Grandfathers.

To John Murray   April 23, 1820

You say that *one half* (of *Don Juan* : presumably Cantos III and IV—R.F.) is very good : you are *wrong* ; for, if it were, it would be the finest poem in existence.

Where is the poetry of which *one half* is good ? is it the
Æneid ? is it *Milton's* ? is it *Dryden's* ? is it any one's
except *Pope's* and *Goldsmith's*, of which *all* is good ? and
yet these two last are the poets your pond poets would
explode. But if *one half* of the two new Cantos be good
in your opinion, what the devil would you have more ?
No—no : no poetry is *generally* good—only by fits and
starts—and you are lucky to get a sparkle here and there.
You might as well want a Midnight *all stars* as rhyme all
perfect.

To PERCY BYSSHE SHELLEY   April 26, 1821

I am very sorry to hear what you say of Keats (who had
died on the previous 23 February—R.F.)—is it *actually*
true (*i.e.*, that his death had been hastened by the *Quarterly*
attack on his poetry—R.F.) ? I did not think criticism
had been so killing. Though I differ from you essentially
in your estimate of his performances, I so much abhor all
unnecessary pain, that I would rather he had been seated
on the highest peak of Parnassus than have perished in
such a manner. Poor fellow ! though with such inordinate
self-love he would probably have not been very happy. I
read the review of *Endymion* in the *Quarterly*. It was
severe,—but surely not so severe as many reviews in that
and other journals upon others.

I recollect the effect on me of the *Edinburgh* on my first
poem ; it was rage, and resistance, and redress—but not
despondency nor despair. I grant that those are not
amiable feelings ; but, in this world of bustle and broil,
and especially in the career of writing, a man should
calculate upon his powers of *resistance* before he goes into
the arena. . . .

I have published a pamphlet on the Pope controversy,
which you will not like. Had I known that Keats was dead
—or that he was alive and so sensitive—I should have
omitted some remarks upon his poetry, to which I was
provoked by his *attack* upon *Pope*, and my disapprobation
of *his own* style of writing.

You want me to undertake a great poem—I have not the
inclination nor the power. As I grow older, the indiffer-

nce—*not* to life, for we love it by instinct—but to the
timuli of life, increases.

To JOHN MURRAY   September 12, 1821

If ever I *do* return to England (which I shan't though),
will write a poem to which *English Bards*, etc., shall be
New Milk, in comparison. Your present literary world of
mountebanks stand in need of such an Atavar ; but I am
not yet quite bilious enough : a season or two more, and a
provocation or two, will wind me up to the point, and then,
have at the whole set !

I have no patience with the sort of trash you send me
out by the way of books ; except Scott's novels, and three
or four other things, I never saw such work or works.
Campbell is lecturing, Moore idling, Southey twaddling,
Wordsworth driveling, Coleridge muddling, Joanna
Baillie piddling, Bowles quibbling, squabbling and
sniveling. Milman will *do*, if he don't cant too much, nor
imitate Southey : the fellow has poesy in him ; but he is
envious, and unhappy, as all the envious are. Still he is
among the best of the day. Barry Cornwall will do better
by and bye, I dare say, if he don't get spoilt by green tea,
and the praises of Pentonville and Paradise Row. The pity
of these men is, that they never lived either in *high life*, nor
in *solitude* : there is no medium for the knowledge of the
busy or the *still* world. If admitted into high life for a
season, it is merely as *spectators*—they form no part of the
Mechanism thereof. Now Moore and I, the one by
circumstances, and the other by birth, happened to be free
of the corporation, and to have entered into its pulses and
passions, *quarum partes fuimus*. Both of us have learnt
by this much which nothing else could have taught us.